THE EMERGING LEADER

Nurturing Your Inner Potential

Srinivas Saripalli

INDIA • SINGAPORE • MALAYSIA

ISBN
Hardcase 979-8-89133-601-8
Paperback 979-8-89067-702-0

Contents

Chapter 1

Introduction

Close your eyes for a moment and imagine a 17-year-old boy from a small town in Odisha, India. He's passionate, ambitious, and brimming with innovative ideas. Now, fast forward a few years, and this very same boy now aged 24 becomes the youngest billionaire in India as his brainchild, OYO Rooms emerges as a multi-billion-dollar startup. Ritesh's journey to success, much like your own, was not without its share of hurdles.

In today's fast-paced, ever-evolving world, the challenges faced by millennials and Gen-Z seem to multiply by the minute. As India's vibrant and dynamic younger generation, you have the power to redefine leadership and create a brighter future for all. But like the captivating story of Ritesh's glorious triumph, your journey to success can be riddled with twists, turns, and obstacles.

12 common traps often hold you back, much like navigating the bustling streets of your city during rush hour. By understanding these traps, you'll be better equipped to steer clear of them and pave your way to becoming the trailblazing leader you're destined to be. So, like Ritesh once did, prepare yourself for this journey. Grab a cup of steaming chai, settle in, and let's embark on

this exciting voyage of self-discovery and transformation together!

- **Perfectionism:** In the wise words of Voltaire, "Perfect is the enemy of good." Embrace this wisdom, and strive for improvement, not perfection. Just like the never-ending quest for the perfect cup of chai, seeking perfection can leave you feeling unsatisfied and demotivated.

  For instance, Ritesh's journey wasn't about creating the perfect hospitality model overnight. It was about making consistent progress. Remember, progress over perfection is the key!

- **Fear of Failure:** Ritesh faced numerous rejections before achieving success. Like a cricketer facing a googly, he too had his stumps rattled several times, but he learned from each failure and came back stronger. Draw inspiration from his story, embrace the failures, and learn from them to become a better player in the game of life.

- **Procrastination:** "Kal karenge" (we'll do it tomorrow) might be your go-to mantra, but pushing things to the last minute can lead to stress and missed opportunities.

  Ritesh's timely actions and decisions, such as the pivot from Oravel Stays to OYO Rooms, prevented stress and missed opportunities in his dream venture. It is an ideal lesson on why it is not fruitful to subscribe to the"kal karenge" mantra.

- **Comparison Trap:** With social media constantly bombarding us with everyone else's highlight reels, it's easy to feel inadequate. But life isn't a race to Keep

Up with the Sharmas. Don't compare your journey with others. Your path is unique, just like you.

- **Digital Distraction:** Today, we are a digitally immersed generation and it provides us with resources to harness the power of technology. While we have grown up to be digital natives, it is crucial to be mindful of digital distractions and prevent the same.

  It is the digital era that empowered success stories including Ritesh's. Ritesh harnessed the power of technology to build his business, but he never let it replace his real-world interactions and connections.

- **Impostor Syndrome:** If you're constantly doubting your achievements and fearing you'll be exposed as a fraud, don't worry, you're not alone. Learn to embrace your wins. It's time to kick this uninvited guest out of your mental house party!

- **Multitasking Myth:** Juggling multiple tasks may feel like a superpower, but it's more like trying to balance on a unicycle while juggling flaming torches. Let's focus on single-tasking and watch your productivity soar.

- **Fear of Conflict:** Disagreeing with others can be as uncomfortable as a family debate on politics, but it's an essential part of growth. Embrace diverse opinions and learn the art of constructive communication.

- **Comfort Zone:** Like a cozy blanket on a chilly winter evening, our comfort zone feels safe and warm. But to grow and thrive, it's time to step out of that cocoon and face new challenges head-on.

- **Redefining Success:** Talking to the graduating students of IIM Nagpur in April 2023, Ritesh Agarwal shared an invaluable lesson that he always held close to his heart: The more successful you become in life, the more rooted you should be.

  If you're still chasing the traditional markers of success like wealth, fame, and status, it's time to hit the brakes and realign your values to think about where the roots of your dream lie. What truly matters to you in life?

- **FOMO (Fear of Missing Out):** Constantly feeling like you're missing out on something better? Instead of letting FOMO take the driver's seat, let's focus on being present and enjoying what life has to offer.

- **Entitlement:** Believing that the world owes you something can lead to disappointment and strained relationships. Time to embrace responsibility, empathy, and emotional intelligence.

We began with the story of a small-town boy, this story is not just about his meteoric rise to the zenith of success. It's a testament to the power of resilience, the courage to dream big, and the will to transform those dreams into reality. Ritesh Agarwal's journey brilliantly encapsulates the 12 notorious traps that can hold you back from achieving your full potential and how each of these traps can be conquered. Like Ritesh, let's embrace the challenges, rewrite the rules, and shape our own stories of success. After all, every trailblazer was once a traveler who dared to take the road less traveled. Your time is now; let's get started!

Chapter 2

Perfectionism – The Elusive Chai

A simmering pot of chai, its irresistible dance of spices, milk, and tea leaves, brews to form the lifeline of India's day-to-day rhythm. Have you ever set out on the monumental quest to create that perfect, flawless cup of chai? The one that strikes the precise balance of sweetness, spice, and that elusive je ne sais quoi? If you've dared to embark on this journey, you've likely experienced the sigh of frustration, the sense of being perpetually on the brink, yet never quite there. Well, my friends, that is perfectionism in a nutshell.

Just like the relentless pursuit of the perfect chai, perfectionism can leave you feeling spent, unfulfilled, and endlessly chasing a mirage. The snares of perfectionism are manifold - it not only ignites unnecessary stress and burnout, but it can also cripple your courage to take risks and seize opportunities. When you're fixated on flawlessness, you risk losing sight of the journey's charm, the unpredictable twists and turns that create the story of your life.

Instead, let's celebrate the sheer joy of moving forward, and unshackle ourselves from the burden of perfection. The magic lies in embracing the beauty of imperfection, absorbing the lessons life offers, and continuously refining your skills. Dare to venture into the unknown, welcome failure as a mentor, and take pride in your achievements, no matter how small they may seem. That, after all, is the true essence of success.

Now, let's delve into what can liberate you from the relentless pursuit of perfection:

Aim for Progress, not Perfection

One of the most compelling stories that underscore this ethos of embracing progress over perfection comes from the vibrant start-up scene of India. It's the story of Ritesh Malik, the dynamic entrepreneur behind Innov8, a revolutionary co-working startup.

When Ritesh first conceived the idea for Innov8, he didn't have a 'perfect' business plan carved out. He didn't wait for an ideal moment when all the stars would align to give him a sure-shot path to success. Instead, he plunged into the chaotic, unpredictable world of startups, driven by a compelling vision and a willingness to learn.

In the early stages, Innov8 was fraught with challenges, as is the case with any disruptive idea. There were logistical hurdles, operational issues, and the mammoth task of building a brand in an already crowded market. A perfectionist approach would have left Ritesh stuck at the drawing board, endlessly tweaking plans and waiting for a flawless execution blueprint.

But Ritesh was different. He understood that in the real world, perfection is a mirage. So, instead of chasing this mirage, he chose to focus on progress - on taking concrete steps, however small, toward his vision. He learned from the chaos, adapted his strategies based on his experiences, and constantly improved his offering.

And the results were nothing short of remarkable. Innov8 gradually carved a niche for itself, providing a flexible, creative workspace solution for businesses and entrepreneurs across India. It not only survived but thrived amidst the chaos, eventually catching the eye of OYO, which acquired it in 2019.

Ritesh's journey is a powerful testament to how progress and adaptation, not perfection, are the keys to success. Embracing imperfections, learning from them, and steadily moving forward can lead to outcomes far more rewarding than what a blinkered pursuit of perfection can offer. So, as we navigate our paths, let's carry with us the spirit of Ritesh's journey, celebrating every small victory, learning from every setback, and above all, cherishing the adventure that is the journey itself.

Embrace Failure

When you think of failure, what comes to mind? Is it a feeling of disappointment, a moment of embarrassment, or perhaps a sudden onset of self-doubt? Like the unexpected lashing of an Indian monsoon, failure can sometimes leave you drenched, unprepared, and gasping for breath. But what if we reframe our perspective and see failure not as an adversary, but as an unexpected mentor?

Let's turn to the cricket pitch and dive into the inspiring story of Shafali Verma, the young Indian cricket sensation.

As a young girl, Shafali harbored a dream - a dream to play for India. But the journey towards her dream wasn't without its trials. The first bump in her road came when she was rejected from a cricket academy when she was a girl. She viewed this setback as a challenge to be surmounted. She disguised as a boy to enroll in the academy and pave the way ahead for her dreams. This was her first trial where she had to battle the biases of a society.

Life, however, had more lessons in store for her. A few years later Shafali was playing in the crucial final of the Women's T20 World Cup 2020. Early into Australia's batting, she missed a catch that allowed Alyssa Healy to score a match-winning 75 runs. The loss was devastating, the missed catch a glaring failure.

But here's where Shafali's story shines. Instead of drowning in disappointment, she chose to swim through it. She acknowledged her mistake, held it up to the light, and powered through. This failure, this missed catch, didn't eclipse her remarkable performance in the tournament as the highest run-scorer for India. Instead, it added a facet to her journey.

Just like Shafali's story, embracing failure allows us to extract valuable lessons from our missteps. So the next time you face failure, remember her story. Remember that every failure is an opportunity to learn and grow. Don't run from it, don't let it engulf you.

Instead, stand tall, face it, and ask, "What can you teach me?" You might be surprised at how much you can learn from your unexpected mentor, failure.

So, how do we begin learning from our unexpected mentor?

Change your perspective: Don't see failure as a cul-de-sac, but rather a stepping-stone on your path. Confront every setback with the question, "What can I take back from this?"

Embrace self-compassion: Remember, the realm of perfection is a myth. Be your ally when you stumble, and acknowledge the passion you've invested.

Reflect and evolve: Remember, the road to success is often a mosaic of failures, identify what went wrong. Use your newfound knowledge to make changes and grow.

Be persistent: Continue to forge ahead towards your aspirations, even in the face of adversity.

Failures, our unexpected mentor can teach us resilience, fuel our determination, and help us grow both personally and professionally. Each failure is a chance to reassess our approach, to learn, and to come back stronger.

Embrace your Inner Hero

In the grand spectacle of life, we often find ourselves playing the villain, casting shadows of self-doubt and criticism. But it's time to rewrite the script, foster self-compassion, and step into the shoes of our own Bollywood hero, brimming with resilience and radiating positivity.

Here's how you can create your blockbuster:

Embrace your emotions: During life's tumultuous scenes, recognize and validate your feelings. Whether it's sorrow, anger, or disappointment, let them wash over you like the monsoon rains in a Bollywood drama, reminding you that every storm precedes a radiant dawn.

Cultivate self-forgiveness: Remember, even the greatest heroes stumble. Forgive your missteps, viewing them not as failures, but as stepping stones on your path to growth and wisdom.

Speak to yourself with kindness: Replace the harsh voice of self-criticism with the uplifting monologue of a Bollywood hero. Let these empowering affirmations become your dialogue, motivating and inspiring you.

Nurture your self-esteem: Celebrate your unique talents, strengths, and achievements. Applaud your small victories and remind yourself that just like any Bollywood hero, you too are deserving of happiness and success.

Prioritize self-care: Even the most invincible Bollywood heroes need moments of respite between their action-packed sequences. Prioritize rest and rejuvenation to strike a harmonious balance between your professional and personal life.

By fostering self-compassion, you're not only building a robust foundation for growth but also bestowing upon yourself the love and encouragement you deserve. In the epic of your life, remember, no villain is too powerful or obstacle too daunting. Your heroic journey awaits, and it's nothing short of a blockbuster!

Gratitude: The Symphony of Life

Life, in all its complexity and beauty, resonates like a grand symphony, a symphony not confined to grand solos or flawless compositions, but one that celebrates the delicate harmony of everyday moments.

It's about the heartwarming chai at the street-side stall, the laughter echoing with an old friend, and the quiet satisfaction of a task well done. This vibrant symphony of life can be fully appreciated through the lens of gratitude.

Gratitude is about focusing on the notes you've played rather than dwelling on the ones you've missed. It's about appreciating the melodies of your journey, the ebbs and flows, the triumphs and trials, and rejoicing in the diversity of life's music.

But how do we tune into this symphony of life and foster a deep-seated sense of gratitude?

Pen the Symphony: Keep a gratitude journal. Each day, ink down at least three things that made your heart hum, no matter how simple they are. It could be the chirping of birds at dawn, a heartfelt compliment, or a new recipe you aced.

Share the Music: Don't just feel gratitude, express it. Let those who've touched your life, however briefly, know the difference they've made. Your words could be the uplifting melody they need.

Listen to the Now: Practise mindfulness. Immerse yourself in the present moment, let every sound, and every sensation sink in. When you truly engage with the now, you start appreciating the rich tapestry of everyday life.

Turn the Dissonance into Harmony: Life will invariably strike some discordant notes. When faced with challenges, strive to find the silver lining. Even in adversity, there's always something to be grateful for.

Celebrate Your Crescendos: Take pride in your accomplishments, regardless of their scale. Relish in your progress, and your growth, and let it amplify your self-belief and drive.

As you embrace gratitude, you'll find yourself dancing to a different rhythm, one that reverberates with love, joy, and an appreciation of life's intricate symphony. So, tune in to the music of gratitude, and watch your life turn into a wondrous, harmonious masterpiece that celebrates every note, every pause, every crescendo. After all, perfection isn't about a flawless performance; it's about cherishing the music in all its beautiful imperfections.

We've walked through the fog of perfectionism, seeing how it can shadow our spirits and dampen our motivation. We've also realized that our strength lies not in chasing an elusive ideal, but in embracing our journey with all its twists and turns, just as we would savor each sip of our chai, without seeking the 'perfect' taste.

As we pull the curtain on this chapter, let's take a moment to appreciate the grand tapestry of our lives. Much like a well-crafted cup of chai, it's a blend of various spices - moments of joy, days of struggle, lessons learned, and victories earned. It's not always perfect, but it's ours, unique, and deeply meaningful.

Our path is strewn with boulders of mistakes, but it is precisely these obstacles that shape us, and make us resilient. They're like the tea leaves in our chai, bitter on their own but lending a robust flavor to the overall brew.

Consider, once again, the journey of Shafali Verma. She faced her share of disappointments and fell numerous times, yet every fall was a stepping stone, leading her to the peak of her game. It wasn't about the perfect strike or the flawless game, but her relentless pursuit of progress, and her tenacity to rise after each fall. She is a testament to the power of embracing imperfections and the magic of perseverance.

So, as you stride forward in your journey, let go of the quest for perfection. Welcome the stumbles, the uncertain steps, the slightly off-key notes. Let yourself enjoy, explore, and evolve, relishing each step, and each experience. It's not about becoming 'perfect' but growing into the most authentic version of yourself.

In the spirit of the beautiful words of Rumi, "The wound is the place where the light enters you," it's your imperfections that let your unique light shine through. They are the threads that weave your story, the strokes that paint your masterpiece. So, celebrate them, for they are the marks of your journey, the testament to your growth, the spices in your chai of life.

Chapter 3

Fear of Failure – The Googly of Life

In the grand narratives of Greek mythology, featuring deities, brave warriors, and mythical beasts, there stands a creature of unrivaled beauty and resolute spirit - the Phoenix. This majestic bird, adorned in golden and scarlet feathers, is a potent symbol of endurance and rejuvenation. The Phoenix teaches us that triumph can often spring from the ashes of defeat, a lesson that holds profound significance for every individual grappling with failures.

The Phoenix's life is a long and vibrant spectacle. However, as the end of its lifecycle approaches, it doesn't shy away. It gathers aromatic branches and spices, building a pyre for itself. There, it willingly succumbs to the fire, reduced to ashes in a spectacle of self-immolation. It may appear as a tragic end, but the Phoenix's story is far from over.

From the ashes of its previous existence, a new Phoenix emerges, reborn and ready for its new life. It retains the wisdom and lessons from its previous existence but isn't chained to them. Instead, it leverages them to forge a renewed life.

Similarly, we experience setbacks and failures that might shake our confidence and blur our dreams. But remember, with every failure, we gain an opportunity to rise again, learn, evolve, and start anew. This is the Phoenix Principle – the art of turning our failures into the foundation of our success. Let's learn to perceive failure as the Phoenix perceives the fire, as a catalyst for our rebirth and growth. Let's realize that every setback can be a setup for an even grander comeback.

The Enigma of Failure

In the grand ballet of life, success and failure dance in a relentless rhythm, each integral to the beautiful journey we embark on. The story of the Indian space program eloquently illustrates this perpetual paradox.

The launch of a satellite into the cosmos, piercing through the inky blackness, is a proud moment of national triumph. However, behind this spectacle lies a tale of unseen struggles, countless adjustments, and inevitable failures. These failures, unseen by the public eye, are not just stumbling blocks. They are the unsung heroes, shaping the path toward every victorious mission.

So, how can we dance gracefully with failure?

Firstly, Embrace the Inevitable: Accept failure as a vital step on the path to success. Treat it not as a roadblock, but as a detour, directing you towards your potential.

Secondly, Learn and Adapt: Break down your failures to understand what went wrong and what could be improved. This understanding should be used to refine your approach, similar to how the Phoenix uses its ashes to rebuild its existence.

Thirdly, Foster Resilience: Failure might be daunting, but it's also temporary. Let your setbacks become the fuel for your journey toward success, igniting the Phoenix spirit within you.

Lastly, Celebrate Growth: Each failure carries a valuable lesson. Celebrate this growth and evolution, knowing that each lesson brings you closer to your ultimate goal.

When life throws you a curveball, face it with grace and resilience, for it could be the stepping stone toward your victory in the great game of life. Remember, every stumble is but a prelude to your Phoenix moment - a glorious rise from the ashes toward your destined peak.

Rising from Ashes

Having imbibed the intriguing tale of the Phoenix, let's apply this timeless wisdom to our contemporary lives. Just as the Phoenix learns from the ashes of its past, we too can morph our failures into enriching experiences.

Embrace the Flames of Failure: The Phoenix doesn't evade the fire; it welcomes it as a part of its lifecycle. In the same vein, don't evade failure. Accept it as a part of your journey, take responsibility for your mistakes, and view them as opportunities for learning. Remember, it's not the fall that hampers us; it's the fear of falling.

Rise with Resilience: Resilience is the ability to recover from adversity, to rise again from the ashes of defeat - a trait that defines the Phoenix. Cultivate resilience by maintaining positivity, practicing self-care, and keeping your focus on your goals regardless of setbacks.

Learn from the Ashes: Just as the Phoenix uses its ashes as the foundation for its new life, we can use our failures as stepping stones toward success. Reflect on your mistakes, analyze what went wrong, and apply these insights to your future pursuits.

Unleash Your Inner Phoenix: Finally, remember that failure does not define you; it refines you. You are not your mistakes. You are the Phoenix that rises from the ashes of those mistakes, emerging stronger, wiser, and more prepared.

As we navigate through the 21st century, the timeless wisdom of the Phoenix deeply resonates with the inspiring tales of triumph in India. Picture our vibrant nation, pulsating with the spirit of a youthful generation - audacious, fearless, and filled with unbridled enthusiasm.

Every one of these torchbearers is embodying the Phoenix's tale in their unique ways, rising, adapting, and soaring higher, prepared to reshape the world with their dreams.

In the grand scheme of life, where victories and setbacks are intricately woven, let's shed light on some tales of audacious dreamers and historic moments. Like the mythical Phoenix that finds new life in its pyre, these individuals have given life to their dreams amidst their struggles, illuminating a path of inspiration for the young generation of India.

Firstly, let's delve into the realm of art and literature, where words and visuals become a mirror to the soul, and the brushstrokes of failure often create the most profound narratives. Rima Das, a renowned filmmaker from a small village in Assam, is a testament to this truth. Despite facing financial challenges and initial rejection from the industry, Rima didn't allow these hurdles to snuff out her creative spark. Like the Phoenix, she used her setbacks as fuel for her fire, rising above her struggles to create her masterpiece. Today, her films have garnered international acclaim, and her work serves as a poignant reminder of the resilience and creativity that can blossom from adversity.

Next, let's step into the exhilarating world of sports. The canvas of Indian cricket history is painted with numerous moments of triumph that echo a formidable battle against failure. These instances, akin to a phoenix rising from the ashes, inspire us and accentuate the spirit of resilience and fortitude.

A memorable example dates back to the unforgettable Test match at Kolkata's Eden Gardens in 2001 against Australia, often lauded as one of the greatest comebacks in cricket history. The Indian cricket team, at the time grappling with criticism and disappointments, was facing a follow-on enforced by the Australians who held a significant lead. Yet, the phoenix was ready to rise from the ashes. An epic partnership between VVS Laxman and Rahul Dravid transformed an impending defeat into a stunning victory, heralding a new era in Indian cricket.

Jumping further back in time, during the colonial era, the "Parsi Cricket Club" squared off against the English cricket team. The Parsis had experienced numerous defeats at the hands of their British opponents. However, in a memorable match in 1889, they triumphed over the English, marking a significant moment in Indian cricket history. This victory was more than a cricketing achievement; it was a symbolic win against colonial rule, exemplifying courage and resilience.

Consider the unforgettable moment that unfolded during the ICC Cricket World Cup in 1983. The Indian cricket team, considered as underdogs, were up against the titans of cricket - the West Indies - in the grand finale at Lord's. The West Indies were the reigning champions, having won the previous two World Cups, and were favored to take the crown once more.

The Indian team had managed to put up a mere 183 runs on the board, a total that seemed far from challenging against the robust West Indian batting line-up. It looked like a certain defeat was looming large for the Indian team. Yet, they refused to succumb to the apparent inevitability of their failure.

Like the Phoenix primed for its resurrection, the Indian team, under the leadership of Kapil Dev, embraced the challenge head-on. Displaying extraordinary courage, determination, and resilience, they defended their total with a vigor that left spectators and critics alike astounded. Against all odds, India emerged victorious, marking a turning point in Indian cricket history.

This iconic victory was the quintessence of the Phoenix spirit, the ability to embrace failure, rise from the ashes, and soar high toward success. It underlined the power of resilience and self-belief, inspiring generations of cricket aspirants and reaffirming the idea that failures are not endpoints but stepping stones toward glorious triumphs.

These stories, while diverse in their journeys, converge on one powerful theme: the transformation of failure into stepping stones to success. Like the Phoenix, these resilient spirits have risen from their setbacks, reaching new heights. Their stories not only celebrate the power of resilience and perseverance but also serve as an anthem for the indomitable spirit of Indian youth. Remember, their stories are still being written. They continue to rise, adapt, and conquer - embodying the spirit of the Phoenix, just as you can too.

Chapter 4

Procrastination - The Kal Karenge Conundrum

As the golden sun sets below the horizon and twilight embraces the subcontinent, the echoes of a popular refrain permeate the bustling lanes of India, "Kal Karenge" - We'll do it tomorrow. It's a mantra that finds resonance across the nation's diverse tapestry, from the fervent urgency of Mumbai's stock exchanges to the languid calm of Kerala's backwaters. This ubiquitous attitude of delay, this seemingly benign tendency to defer tasks, is the deceptive dragon of procrastination that we so often find ourselves attempting to slay.

Before we ready our swords and shields to conquer this dragon, let's first understand its origins, its roots embedded deep within our psyche. Why do we procrastinate? The answer lies in a labyrinth of psychological and environmental factors. We may fear failure or success, or perhaps even the effort required to attempt the task at hand. Alternatively, we may simply lack interest or motivation, the task appearing as a monotonous mountain rather than a challenge to be surmounted.

Consider the Greek myth of Sisyphus, who was condemned to eternally push a boulder up a hill, only for it to roll down again. Our mundane tasks can often feel like this relentless Sisyphean labor, a monotonous cycle leading to procrastination. However, what if we were to redefine this myth for our context? What if, instead of viewing our tasks as Sisyphus's burden, we perceived them as stepping stones to our goal, as a challenge to be undertaken with joy? Would the boulder still seem as heavy?

As we brace ourselves to vanquish the insidious dragon of procrastination, we must understand that our greatest weapons are not external, but internal – our mental resolve and unwavering determination. Our insight into this pervasive habit becomes the compass guiding our journey from acceptance of its existence to ultimately subduing it.

The Stepping Stones

Visualize standing at the base of a formidable mountain, its pinnacle hidden in the clouds, the path uphill appearing treacherous and strenuous. This mountain symbolizes your task, the mission you've been evading, and the genesis of your procrastination. To conquer this massive impediment, you need to dissect your task into manageable segments, much like chiseling stepping stones out of the mountain's formidable facade. Each stone signifies a minor, feasible goal, a segment of the larger mission.

The Stride Forward

Initiate your climb by taking a single stride, followed by another, acknowledging every small triumph as you ascend. Soon enough, you'll find the once intimidating peak beneath you, and you are basking in the grandeur of your accomplishment.

Sorting Your Stones

Imagine that each of your tasks is a stone of varying sizes scattered on the ground. It's an intimidating sight, to say the least, much like the mountain of procrastination. But how do you make it manageable? Enter prioritization. It's like sifting through these stones and arranging them according to their weight - or in this case, their importance and urgency. Once sorted, it's easier to decide which stone to pick up first and which can wait for later. Prioritization helps you focus on tasks that matter the most, providing a clear roadmap to your goal.

Rolling Your Stones

Remember, a stone gathers no moss when it's in motion. The same applies to your tasks. Once you've begun and gained some momentum, it becomes easier to maintain it. The initial effort of pushing the stone may seem challenging, but as it starts to roll, it naturally gains speed. Think of your tasks as stones that need to start rolling. Overcome the initial inertia, keep them moving, and you'll find it easier to continue the task than to start it anew.

Polishing Your Stones

The stones you have may seem dull and unattractive at first, much like a task you're avoiding. But what if you were to polish them, and add a shine that makes them attractive? This is where your mindset plays a crucial role. Perceiving your tasks positively, as opportunities for learning and growth rather than burdens, can make them more appealing. Like polishing a stone to reveal its hidden luster, a positive mindset uncovers the hidden potential in every task, turning the mundane into the meaningful.

Stacking Your Stones

Now that your stones are sorted, rolling, and polished, it's time to start stacking them. This symbolizes the act of consistently accomplishing your tasks, one after another. Stack a stone each day, and over time, you'll have a sturdy structure symbolizing your victories over procrastination. Remember, consistency is key. A single stone might not make much of a difference, but a stack of stones is a monument to your success.

To drive this point home, let's traverse into the thrilling domain of international entrepreneurship, taking inspiration from the incredible story of Netflix. Founded in 1997 by Reed Hastings and Marc Randolph, Netflix faced the colossal challenge of establishing itself in an evolving market. The founders had a vision - to revolutionize the way people consume media, but the reality of translating this dream into a thriving enterprise was daunting.

However, instead of succumbing to the magnetism of procrastination, they resolved to approach their gargantuan task by dividing it into manageable segments. From creating a distinctive business model, and recruiting a skilled team, to introducing an innovative DVD-by-mail service, they tackled each stage with an unyielding focus.

The journey was fraught with uncertainties, but each obstacle was viewed not as a roadblock but as stepping stones guiding them toward their goal.

Today, Netflix is a titan in the streaming industry, boasting over 200 million subscribers worldwide. Its success story serves as a powerful testament to the efficacy of our strategy against procrastination - the impact of breaking down a mammoth task into feasible steps and making steady progress toward success. The evolution of Netflix is a compelling reminder that even the most intimidating of tasks can be conquered, one stepping stone at a time.

Speaking of the joy of achievement and overcoming daunting odds, let's turn our gaze towards a young Indian trailblazer who has etched his name in golden letters in the annals of Indian sports history - Neeraj Chopra. Neeraj, an Indian track and field athlete, was the quintessential dreamer. Born in a small village in Haryana, he was far removed from the world of international sports. However, his dreams weren't bound by his circumstances. His aspirations soared higher than the javelin he would one day master.

His journey, however, was not devoid of challenges. There were setbacks, disappointments, and there were moments of procrastination too. The steep path towards his goal sometimes seemed insurmountable, echoing the 'Kal Karenge' syndrome. But Neeraj chose to rise above it. He decided to embrace the challenge, look beyond the mountainous task, and break it down into manageable stepping stones. Each day of training, each throw of the javelin, and each victory at a local level was a stepping stone towards his ultimate goal. It was his 'Aaj Karenge' moment that he chose to live, day after day.

The results were nothing short of phenomenal. Neeraj Chopra went on to make India proud by bagging a gold medal in Javelin throw at the 2020 Tokyo Olympics, a first in India's athletic history. His journey serves as a shining testament to the power of overcoming procrastination, breaking tasks into manageable goals, and the magic that unfurls when 'Kal Karenge' transforms into 'Aaj Karenge'.

As we bask in the glory of such inspiring journeys, let's equip ourselves to slay the dragon of procrastination. Our arsenal does not demand swords and shields; instead, it yearns for a change of perspective, a strategic approach, and an iron resolve. So, as we stand at the foot of our mountains, let's remember Neeraj Chopra and countless other trailblazers. Let's break down our tasks into stepping stones, relish each small victory, and march forward with unwavering resolve. For it is then, in that precious moment of action, that the deceptive dragon of procrastination is vanquished, giving birth to the resplendent phoenix of productivity. And as this phoenix takes flight, it illuminates our path, guiding us from the realm of 'Kal Karenge' to the vibrant land of 'Aaj Karenge'.

Chapter 5

Comparison Trap – The Great Indian Race

In a world that pulsates to the rhythm of a thousand heartbeats, where every moment is woven into the great tapestry of human experience, there exists a realm that thrives on brevity and immediacy - the kingdom of social media. Here, on the grand stages of Instagram, Facebook, and Twitter, we play out the scripts of our lives, casting and recasting ourselves in a multitude of roles. Yet, in this parade of carefully crafted narratives, we find ourselves entranced by a mirage - a shimmering illusion of perfection that impacts our self-esteem and mental health.

The first act of this tale unfurls in the labyrinth of Likes, Comments, and Shares. A 'like' is not merely a click; it's an affirmation, a validation, a fleeting shot of dopamine. It's the currency of our digital persona, and in its pursuit, we often stake our self-esteem. The surge in popularity becomes a measurement of our worthiness, subtly influencing our mental well-being.

Let's dive deeper into this mirage. Picture a bustling digital bazaar where everyone is selling their best lives - vacation selfies from exotic locations, success stories, perfect relationships, and tales of unending happiness. Consuming this continuous reel of highlights, it's natural to question the ordinariness of our lives. This spectacle, though enchanting, can stir a whirlpool of anxiety and loneliness, pulling us into its depths where we're left juggling our insecurities and doubts.

In the second act, we encounter the twin illusions of connectivity and comparison. The paradox of feeling alone in a 'connected' world can lead to a skewed self-image, fueling the vicious cycle of low self-esteem and mental health issues.

Yet, as we stand entranced by this mirage, it's important to remember that it's a construct, a masterfully crafted illusion. To navigate through this maze, we need to arm ourselves with awareness and discernment. This is the first step in disentangling our self-worth from the snares of social media validation and escaping the comparison trap.

Let us turn our gaze to the radiant tale of Alicia Souza, an Indian illustrator, whose life sparkles with the enchantment of her evocative artistry. Alicia, a wellspring of infectious vitality, is a beacon in the realms of creativity, her warmth and humor seeping into her delightfully candid illustrations. She co-founded and breathed life into Chumbak, a thriving lifestyle brand, before choosing to follow the call of her passion — illustrating the symphony of everyday life.

In Alicia's whimsical doodles, we see life, not in its picture-perfect glory, but in its authentic, undiluted form. Alicia's canvas isn't reserved for grandiose feats or ethereal beauty; it thrives on the ordinary and the everyday. Through her art, she radiates positivity, gently nudging her vast online community towards acceptance of our collective humanness — the stumbles, the mundane, the ordinary. Her creative journey stands as a powerful testament to using social media, not as a gilded mirror reflecting curated perfection but as a clear window, revealing the charm in authenticity.

Alicia's story unfolds a vibrant tapestry, where social media transcends its superficial role as an approval-seeking tool, morphing into a platform that celebrates individuality, impacts positively, and cherishes authenticity. Our dance with social media can transform, shifting from a grueling marathon of comparison to a jubilant jive of personal growth and self-expression.

The practice of gratitude, often overlooked in the heady rush of digital interactions, can serve as an anchor, grounding us amidst the ever-churning sea of social media. Envision a day caught unawares in a sudden downpour. Many would regard it as a stroke of misfortune, but through the lens of gratitude, it morphs into a beautiful symphony of raindrops, the scent of petrichor, and nature's sigh of relief to the parched earth. It's this very shift in perspective that colors our world differently, making our half-empty glass appear half-full.

Now imagine carrying this transformative lens into our digital lives. Gratitude nudges us to cherish our unique journey, rather than covet someone else's path. It invites us to celebrate every milestone, irrespective of its size, instead of being overshadowed by the magnified successes of others. Gratitude teaches us that the beauty of life lies in the journey and not just the destination.

The journey towards gratitude and personal growth is exemplified by Bretman Rock, a 24-year-old Filipino social media star. Bretman shot to fame on Vine and YouTube with a vivacious personality that brought sunshine to the often monotonous feed. He poured colors into the world of beauty and fashion content, demonstrating a unique sense of style that was as bold as his personality. What truly set him apart was his unwavering commitment to authenticity, LGBTQ+ solidarity, and self-expression.

Despite the whirlwind of fame and influence, Bretman remained grounded, often expressing his gratitude for his journey and the experiences that sculpted his vibrant persona. He broke barriers by becoming the face of Nike's Pride campaign and working with renowned designers like Michael Kors and Stella McCartney, all while staying true to himself. Making history, he graced the cover of Playboy in 2021, the first openly gay male to do so.

Bretman's journey serves as a beacon of inspiration, exemplifying that success lies not in conforming to societal standards but in embracing and expressing one's authentic self. His attitude of gratitude, despite the highs and lows of his journey, reminds us of the importance of acknowledging and appreciating our paths. Through his story, we realize that the stage of social media can be transformed from a space of comparison to a platform of authenticity and gratitude. It's this shift that allows us to grow, evolve, and blossom in the grand theatre of life.

In the orchestra of our lives, where every note matters, personal growth finds its rhythm in a growth mindset - the belief that our abilities can be nurtured through effort, learning, and resilience. This mindset transforms the competitive race into a journey of self-improvement, where we strive to outdo ourselves rather than others. Here are pointers that will help you through this unique and transformative journey:

Embracing an Abundance Mindset

The first step to cultivating gratitude is transitioning our mindset from one of scarcity to abundance. Consider the vast expanses of experiences, relationships, and personal strengths you have at your disposal. Like Alicia Souza who transformed the vast canvas of social media into a space for her whimsical illustrations, treats these platforms as a vibrant panorama that expands horizons rather than a restrictive cage that shrinks self-worth.

The Gratitude Journal

Initiate the habit of recording your everyday joys in a gratitude journal. This could range from a shared moment of laughter, the first sip of your morning coffee, or the vibrant hues of a sunset. This simple act of acknowledging and documenting these positive instances helps in ingraining them in your consciousness and reinforces your sense of gratitude.

The Art of Mindful Consumption

Every morsel we consume on social media leaves an imprint on our minds. Choose wisely. Be the curator of your own social media feed. Allow only those accounts that inspire you, encourage positivity, and align with your growth path.

Reconnecting with Reality

Scheduling regular periods of digital detox allows you to form a deeper connection with yourself and your surroundings. This intentional break can help recalibrate your perspective, making space for gratitude, and drawing attention to the tangible beauty around you.

The Shift from Comparison to Appreciation

Whenever you find yourself on the precipice of comparison, intentionally make a conscious shift towards appreciation. Celebrate the achievements of others, just as we admire the vibrant brushstrokes on an artist's canvas. This not only prevents the plunge into the abyss of negativity but also fosters a sense of communal celebration.

Expressing Gratitude

Let your social media platforms be the loudspeakers that amplify your gratitude. Share the positives, the moments of joy, the victories however small, and express thanks to those who have contributed to your journey.

Setting Goals

Chart out your growth journey with a constellation of achievable goals. Ensure that these goals resonate with your passions, values, and aspirations, serving as the guiding North Star in your journey toward personal growth.

Celebrating Progress: Every Step Counts

A celebration should not be reserved for the end of the journey. Every step forward, regardless of how small, is progress worth celebrating.

Embrace Lifelong Learning

Just as the river continually shapes the stone, let every encounter, and every experience sculpt you. Embrace the journey of learning as an ongoing process. Treat triumphs and setbacks alike as teachers offering valuable lessons.

Authenticity: Your Unique Signature

The most important step of all - stay true to who you are. Authenticity is your unique signature, the essence of your being that distinguishes you from the crowd. As Alicia Souza's illustrations resonate with her audience due to their authentic reflection of life, let your narrative, both on and off social media, be an authentic representation of who you truly are.

Social media, in the grand ballet of life, is but a prop. Its influence — whether it amplifies the hollow echoes of comparison or reverberates the harmonious notes of authenticity — is orchestrated by the melody we choose to strike. After all, the stage is ours, and the rhythm of the symphony rests in our hands.

Chapter 6

Digital Distractions – A Double-Edged Sword

In the not-so-distant past, a revolution unfurled silently, yet with the momentum of a tidal wave. It was the dawn of the Digital Age. In this momentous upheaval, the human race catapulted itself into a realm that was the stuff of science fiction just decades ago. A place where information became omnipresent, barriers dissolved like mist, and voices traveled farther than the most daring explorers of yore. We had entered the digital universe – our modern-day Atlantis.

Picture this: a young woman in Mumbai, as she brings to life a startup that was but a seedling of imagination, only because she could access knowledge at a lightning pace and without boundaries. Or a teenager in a sleepy town whose art, once confined to the pages of a sketchbook, now gains adoration from all corners of the world. They are the natives of this Digital Atlantis, sailing the seas of limitless possibilities.

But hold that frame. As we delve deeper, there's a murmur, a slow hum, which soon amplifies into a cacophony. It's the other side, the underbelly of this limitless cosmos. The vortex.

Our explorer is caught. The very waves that propelled his dreams are now shackles. Our artist looks up, and the world is a blur. The screen, once a window, now demands her every waking moment.

This, my friends, is the double-edged sword - the Paradox of Digital Consumption. The digital universe, boundless and brimming with treasures, is also an abyss that can suck you into a black hole of lost time, strained eyes, and phantom vibrations. Here, dragons and demons are cloaked not in scales, but in notifications, likes, and retweets. They gnaw at your time and feed on your attention.

To navigate these waters is to be an explorer in the truest sense. The compass and the astrolabe you need are discernment and balance. The treasure is not just the pearls of information and connection, but the wisdom to know when to close the treasure chest, to resurface, breathe the air, and live in a tangible world.

As we resurface from the depths of this Digital Atlantis, the air is crisp and fresh. We've beheld the treasures and navigated the abyss. But the journey doesn't end here; it's only just begun. With our chests full of digital pearls, we have the power to chart our course. But how do we stave off the sirens and sea monsters that beset our path? How do we ensure that the treasures don't turn into anchors pulling us down? It's here that we must become alchemists, turning the digital bounty into golden moments of real life.

Enter the realm of the Healthy Digital Diet.

Think of your mind as a sanctuary. The information you consume is the bricks and mortar with which you build this sacred space. It's imperative to select these with care. The digital world has given us access to boundless materials – but it's up to us to choose between the marbles and the pebbles.

Too much of anything, even the most precious material, can create an impenetrable wall around us. We need to build windows – windows that give us a view of the world beyond the digital. The right digital diet is about finding the balance – that perfect symmetry between the digital and the physical that allows us to create bridges, not walls.

Our hearts must not race at every ping; our minds should not be haunted by the shadows of unchecked notifications. We must keep our sanctuary pristine, invulnerable to the tempests of digital excess.

Now, you might wonder: how do we achieve this balance? How do we become the architects of our sanctuaries and the masters of our digital destinies?

Identifying Consumption Patterns

First and foremost, we need to hold a mirror to our digital consumption. What are we consuming and in what quantities? Much like understanding the constituents of the food that grace our plates, it is crucial to discern the nature of the content we consume.

Take Action: Keep a log for a week, jot down what you did each time you unlocked your phone. Did you learn something new, or did you simply fall into the rabbit hole of an endless feed? The revelations may astonish you.

The Rule of Thirds: Crafting a Balanced Digital Palette

In photography, the rule of thirds is used to capture balanced and engaging images. Similarly, applying this rule to your screen time can bring balance. Divide your digital time into thirds: one for productivity, one for learning, and one for entertainment.

Take Action: Analyze your typical screen time and adjust it to fit this structure. The balance will ensure that while you indulge in some entertainment, you are also growing and accomplishing meaningful work.

Employing Apps to Rein in the Digital Horses

Ironically, the very devices that often serve as conduits for overindulgence can be harnessed to foster moderation. There's an app for everything, including reining in on excessive usage. They are the leashes that prevent the stallions of digital distraction from bolting.

Take Action: Try apps like Freedom or StayFocusd. Set limits for how much time you want to spend on specific sites or apps. When you reach your limit, these sentinels will lock you out.

The 5-Minute Rule: The Sprints of Digital Engagement

Constant marathons of screen time can be exhausting. Instead, try short sprints. The 5-minute rule involves engaging with a digital platform for just five minutes and then taking a break.

Take Action: Set a timer for 5 minutes for any non-essential digital task. Once it goes off, step away, and do something else for a bit. It's short enough to prevent fatigue but long enough to stay updated.

Creating Digital Curfews: The Night Watchmen of Attention

There's a reason townsfolk of the past had night watchmen and curfews – to ensure safety and security. In the digital world, our attention needs a safeguard too. Setting digital curfews, especially around bedtime, can be a game-changer for mental peace and sleep quality.

Take Action: Aim to switch off all digital devices an hour before bed. Utilize this time for winding down - perhaps read a book, or engage in a light conversation with family.

Cultivating Mindfulness: The Zen Garden of the Digital Landscape

In the tumultuous waves of information, cultivating a Zen garden through mindfulness can center us. Being aware of our digital interactions and how they affect our mood and productivity is a powerful tool.

Take Action: Practice being present during your digital engagements. How do you feel? Is this making you happy, anxious, or neutral? Being aware can guide your choices in the digital world.

Human Connections: The Pillars of the Parthenon

In the digital age, as towering as the Parthenon, don't forget the pillars that hold it up - human connections. While technology connects us globally, nothing replaces the warmth of a face-to-face conversation or the strength gained from a friend's embrace.

Take Action: Schedule regular meetups with friends or family, even if it's a brief coffee. Engage in community activities or social groups that align with your interests.

Seeking Professional Help: The Guiding Lighthouse

When the seas are particularly stormy, there's no shame in seeking the guiding light of a lighthouse – professional help. If you find that despite your best efforts, the digital world is taking a toll on your well-being, don't hesitate to seek guidance.

Take Action: Consult a psychologist or counselor who specializes in digital addiction or related issues. Sometimes an outside perspective can be the beacon you need.

In the matrix of the digital realm, we can't lose sight of the life pulsating beyond our screens. These are the connections that demand our laughter and tears; our touch, our presence, and our undivided attention - they are what make life vibrant, textured, and deeply fulfilling.

Think about the last time you shared a hearty laugh with a friend, felt the grass between your toes, or observed the world through your lens, not through the lens of a camera. These experiences are the jewels of human existence, and they await us with open arms.

This, however, is not a plea for a digital exodus; technology has knit the world closer. It's a clarion call to infuse our digital interactions with the warmth of our offline lives. To look up from our screens, to be there – wholly, unabashedly. To listen to a friend without the pings governing our conversation, to relish a meal without the pressing need to curate it for the world, to allow ourselves the luxury of immersion in a book, a song, a moment.

For instance, let's delve into the world of book clubs – a space where literary aficionados come together. Today, book clubs have proliferated across digital platforms. Imagine the sheer beauty of taking these conversations from the screen to your living room, a cozy café, or a lush park. The digital sparks the connection, but the real world nurtures it. The animated discussions, the exchange of paperbacks, the scent of pages mixing with coffee – this is an alchemy that only the offline realm can conjure.

And then, there are the silent reading communities that have blossomed across cities. Chennai Reads, BessyReads, CubbonReads - these are havens for those who find solace in the silent camaraderie of fellow book lovers. There's something profoundly serene about a group of strangers gathered under a canopy of trees, or in the seashores bathed in sunlight, sharing nothing but the silent turning of pages. The absence of small talk, the unspoken bond of bibliophiles – it's almost meditative.

As we forge ahead in the digital era, let's craft our paths with the wisdom that comes from recognizing the essence of balance. Our screens have offered us gateways, but our senses crave the gardens beyond.

In the symphony of life, the notes played off-screen are as vital as those orchestrated in the digital sphere. Let us strike a chord that resonates with the depth and diversity of human connection.

In this delicate dance between the virtual and the real, we find a rhythm that is uniquely our own. Let this rhythm guide you through the boundless spaces of the digital universe, but let it also lead you back home – to the earth, to touch, to the unfathomable depths of the human heart. Through this, we find that the digital and the real are not adversaries, but partners in the wondrous dance that is life.

Chapter 7

Impostor Syndrome – The Uninvited Mental Guest

In the uncharted territories of the mind, there often lurks a shrewd squatter. It slips through the alleys of your thoughts, never asking for permission and never leaving a trace. This shadowy figure insidiously persuades you that you are merely wearing someone else's armor, standing on a podium built for another. It convinces you that the applause that fills the room is not meant for your ears and that you, my friend, are merely a stand-in for the real hero. This whispering phantom is none other than Impostor Syndrome.

Imagine Impostor Syndrome as a master of disguise, a consummate actor. It doesn't just wear one mask; it has an entire wardrobe. It can dress as humility, fear, perfectionism, or relentless critic. It's so adept at blending into the background that often you don't even realize it's part of your mental ensemble. The first battle in ejecting this mental squatter is detecting its presence. It's that nagging voice questioning your merit, the hesitation to claim your achievements and the quaking fear that your façade will crumble. To strip the Impostor of its power, we must first rip off its many masks. Here's your guide to spotting the signs:

Wearing a Mask: Think about the moments when you are playing a role rather than being yourself. Are you constantly in character, shielding your true self because you feel it just doesn't measure up? That mask might be concealing the impostor's grin.

Relentless Perfectionism: Picture this - you're up all night, trying to get that project just right, never satisfied, never done. It's because any tiny flaw feels like it might give you away as a fraud. That endless chase? It's you running from the imposter's shadow.

Shrugging Off Success: So, you nailed a big achievement, but instead of taking a bow, you say it was luck or good timing. Take notice if you are dismissive when praise comes your way. This isn't modesty speaking; it's the impostor talking you out of owning your achievements.

Living in Fear of Being 'Found Out': That nagging feeling that someone is about to tap you on the shoulder and tell you that the jig is up, that you don't belong here, that you never did. This persistent anxiety is like the impostor syndrome's business card.

It's time to put this sneaky, freeloading tenant on notice. Recognizing these signs is like flipping on the lights in a room the imposter thought it had to itself. Knowing what you're up against is the first step in showing the imposter the door.

Now that you've flicked the lights on, the impostor, like a startled burglar, is looking for a dark corner. But you're not about to let it slink away; you're about to face it down.

Your mind is the arena, and it's high time you had home advantage. Here's how you take control:

Own Your Success: There's a vital distinction between being modest and disowning your achievements. Your successes are not serendipitous accidents; they are the culmination of your skills, efforts, and sometimes, yes, a little bit of luck. But remember, luck is just the result of opportunity meeting preparation. Construct a 'success board' – this can be an actual board with pinned items, or a digital one. Display awards, appreciative emails, a record of risks taken - anything that demonstrates your triumphs. Whenever the impostor whispers, glance at this board. Like Dumbledore said, "Happiness can be found in the darkest of times if one only remembers to turn on the light."

Seek External Perspectives: There's a saying that "a doctor who treats himself has a fool for a patient." Sometimes, we are so embroiled in our thoughts that we become blind judges of our worth. This is when you need to turn to your jury - friends, family, or mentors. They are mirrors reflecting your genuine self. Share your fears and apprehensions. More often than not, they will provide you with the perspective you need. Their words can become your armor.

Set Realistic Goals: Mount Everest wasn't conquered in a day. It takes acclimatization, climbing smaller peaks, and understanding that sometimes you need to descend a little to ascend successfully. Translate that into your life. Set yourself achievable goals. They should be challenging enough to stretch you but not so ambitious that they are intimidating. And don't forget to celebrate the small victories. Whether it's a project well done or a day where you contributed positively to someone's life - these small wins build the momentum that fuels confidence.

Reframe Your Thoughts: Your brain is an astonishing organ. It's also surprisingly plastic, capable of being molded. So, rewire it! When you catch yourself thinking, "I am not good enough," challenge it! Would an impostor be invited to give a talk on a subject they know nothing about? No! Just as an athlete trains their body, train your mind. Practice positive affirmations – write them down, if it helps. Speak to yourself in front of the mirror. It might seem silly, but it's you coaching yourself into a winning mentality.

The Rise of Sundar Pichai

Imagine a young boy in Chennai, India, in a house without a television and only a rotary telephone. The idea that he would one day helm a company that is the epitome of the internet age could not have been further from his reality. But this is where the journey of Sundar Pichai began.

As Pichai progressed through his education and career, climbing the ranks from engineer to executive, the weight of expectation and the magnitude of his responsibilities began to take a toll. Sundar Pichai, though extraordinary in his achievements, confessed to having moments where he felt like he didn't quite belong in the rooms where the world's technological future was being decided.

In a candid admission, Pichai spoke about grappling with impostor syndrome, especially early in his career. The illustrious corridors of Stanford and Silicon Valley made him question his place amongst such an elite cohort.

But what did Pichai do to shrug off this mental shackle?

He focused on the value he brings. He realized that his unique perspective, hailing from a humble background, offered something special. He didn't have to be like everyone else; he had to be Sundar. By embracing his roots and leveraging his knack for product innovation, he became an indispensable part of Google, leading him to be its CEO.

Take a moment to fathom this - the boy from Chennai who shared a modest living space with his family now spearheads an entity that shapes how the world accesses information.

From the gleaming corridors of Google's headquarters, let's step through the tapestry of time and words into the library of one of the most celebrated and controversial authors of our age, Salman Rushdie.

Born in Bombay, India, Rushdie grew up in a Muslim family and later moved to the UK. His early life was a canvas painted with diverse cultures, a confluence of Eastern heritage and Western enlightenment. But this amalgamation also became the crucible for a great internal conflict.

Rushdie's audacious storytelling is known to intertwine myth, reality, and a sprinkle of magical realism. His words soared, but not without turbulence. "Midnight's Children" heralded his arrival into literary stardom, winning the Man Booker Prize. However, it was "The Satanic Verses" that marked a cataclysmic turning point in his life.

The book led to outrage among some quarters in the Muslim community and resulted in a fatwa being issued for his assassination. This was the moment when the voice, which had so profoundly resonated across continents, risked being silenced forever.

And yet, what is seldom talked about is Rushdie's battle with impostor syndrome. Yes, even a literary maestro like him. Amidst the whirlwind of accolades and controversies, he confided in interviews about periods of self-doubt. The very ingenuity that defined his works became the anchor of his internal strife.

What allowed Rushdie to transcend this crippling self-doubt?

He clung to his pen. He found refuge in his words. It was his unyielding commitment to his art that not only sustained him through physical threats but also through the tempests of his mind.

Rushdie believed in the power of stories, and he knew that his voice, though embattled, had a place in the world's literary symphony. He went on to author several more novels, essays, and memoirs, continuing to enchant and challenge his readers.

As we look at Salman Rushdie, standing on a different pinnacle than Sundar Pichai yet facing the same shadows of impostor syndrome, we see a reaffirmation of the indomitable human spirit. From the realm of bits and bytes to the enigmatic universe of words and stories, the journey to overcome self-doubt is a shared one.

As we trace the lines drawn by the likes of Sundar Pichai and Salman Rushdie, we are reminded that the tapestry of our lives is a blend of triumphs, struggles, doubts, and revelations. The impostor within whispers its shadowed untruths not just in the corners of an unknown artist's studio or a fledgling entrepreneur's home office, but also within the echoing halls where legends tread.

But, let it be known that the pages of our stories are ours to pen. The impostor is but an echo of our fears, and we have the ink of resolve and resilience. Own that ink. When the specter of doubt looms, let it not make its abode in your soul. Instead, let it be a reminder, a gentle nudge to rekindle the fire that courses through your veins.

Know this: Greatness is not an antechamber reserved for a preordained few. It is a summit that awaits those who dare to climb, even with trembling hands and self-doubt as companions. The impostor whispers in the ear of the lionhearted, for it knows no place among the timid.

Forge ahead. With each step, may the whispers grow fainter, until the winds of your ascent carry them away, leaving behind only the resonance of your true, unyielding voice.

So, when your time comes to hold your trophy high, be it a manuscript, a groundbreaking invention, a healed soul, or a simple 'well done' from someone you respect, know that you earned it. Stand tall, look impostor syndrome in the eye, and declare: I belong here. My work, my voice, and my essence have a place in this tapestry of stars.

And just like that, the uninvited mental guest will find your soul an unwelcoming sanctuary for its whispers, and the echoing halls within will resound with nothing but the symphony of your triumphs.

Chapter 8

Multitasking Myth – The Juggling Act

Picture a colossal circus tent, bathed in colorful lights, where the energy of the crowd is palpable. Amid this electric atmosphere, there's an agile performer, illuminated under the spotlight, juggling an array of objects: balls, plates, and flaming torches. The audience is captivated, their eyes glued to the whirlwind of motion. But as the act reaches its crescendo, a close observer can see beads of sweat forming on the performer's brow, and the strain etched on his face. The juggling becomes erratic, and soon enough, balls are missed, plates shatter, and the torches flicker out. The crowd, still in the thrall of what seemed like an impossible feat, now comes to a stark realization - the spectacle had its limits.

This riveting scene is a metaphor for the allure and pitfalls of multitasking in our lives.

In today's fast-paced society, multitasking is often heralded as a superpower. It's become a badge of honor to declare how we can type out emails during meetings, skim through reports while on calls, and keep multiple social media tabs open. This juggling act feeds into an illusion of being ultra-productive.

However, just like the circus performer, there's a breaking point.

Now, let's don the lab coats and peek at the science behind it. Studies in cognitive psychology have shed light on an eye-opening truth: what we consider multitasking is the brain switching between tasks at breakneck speed. Imagine a ping-pong match where the ball is being hit back and forth rapidly; that's your brain trying to keep up. It doesn't genuinely process multiple tasks in unison. Instead, there's a constant back-and-forth, and this takes a toll. Each switch carries a cognitive cost, referred to as 'attention residue'. This residue muddles your focus, leads to errors, and heightens stress.

Now that we've unmasked the illusion, let's set our sights on an alternative approach that is both sustainable and rewarding: single-tasking.

Think of your brain as the captain of a ship navigating through tumultuous seas. Multitasking is akin to being tossed and turned by every wave and gust of wind. In contrast, single-tasking is like having a well-calibrated compass and a clear chart. Your ship moves purposefully, undeterred by the distractions that storm around you.

Ask yourself this - which approach is likely to reach the destination efficiently and with the least damage?

Imagine the moment your brain locks its crosshairs on a single task; it's akin to donning high-precision blinders. The cacophony of the outer world diminishes, and you are left with an unadulterated focus. But the enchantment doesn't stop at merely blocking out distractions - something remarkable is happening within the recesses of your brain. Molecules are in motion, and certain regions, especially the prefrontal cortex, spark into action like an expert conductor leading an orchestra. Visualize the prefrontal cortex as the first mate, meticulously plotting a path through tempestuous waters.

Now, let's venture into the realm of multitasking. Here, your brain morphs into a frenzied ping-pong player, the ball darting back and forth with relentless fervor. Your mind doesn't truly multitask; it merely swaps tasks with alarming speed. This frantic switching isn't free – it extracts a toll. Imagine a car changing gears incessantly; the engine judders, losing both momentum and efficiency.

In contrast, single-tasking harnesses your brain's resources into a concentrated beam of focus. It's the stark difference between the erratic spattering of rain and the potent, directed stream from a firehose. Here's the astounding part - research demonstrates that by dedicating your attention to a single task, your proficiency can skyrocket by up to 50%, and you achieve this in 40% less time. It's like trading in your old bicycle for a state-of-the-art jet.

Picture a software developer, let's call him Alex, entrenched in creating a groundbreaking application. When he's singularly absorbed, every keystroke is purposeful, every line of code a stroke of art. His thoughts flow like a well-charted river, and the elements synchronize flawlessly.

Now, imagine Alex juggling coding, emails, and incessant notifications. It resembles wading through a quagmire – each step is labored, the grace is lost, and frustration mounts.

Think of your brain as a gourmet pie. The pie is sumptuous, but it can only be sliced in so many ways.

Single-tasking is like dedicating the entire, delectable pie to one sublime dish. Have you savored a pie where every ingredient melded perfectly, and it was baked to perfection? The taste is transcendent. That's the caliber of performance you achieve when you dedicate yourself to single-tasking – sheer excellence.

Single-tasking transcends the act of completing tasks; it is an homage to the craft. It is the commitment of your essence to the moment, whether you are conjuring a painting, unraveling a scientific mystery, or engrossed in conversation. When you focus, you are not just doing something; you are fully living in the tapestry of the moment. Your brain is not merely an organ; it's an instrument, and single-tasking is how you play it to compose the symphonies of your achievements.

Let's steer our gaze toward a virtuoso who has transformed the world of music production through the sheer intensity of his focus – the legendary Rick Rubin. His portfolio reads like a who's who of the music industry, having caressed the chords alongside giants such as Johnny Cash, Jay-Z, and the Red Hot Chili Peppers. What sets Rubin on a pedestal is not solely his acute sense of melody but his indomitable devotion to the very essence of creativity. Picture a bustling trading floor, brokers juggling phone calls and screens. Now, replace that image with the soothing aura of a Zen garden. Rick Rubin is the Zen master amidst a cacophony, wielding focus like a sacred blade of old.

Visualize the pulsating heart of a recording studio with Rick Rubin orchestrating the flow. There's a reverence in the air that parallels the sacred silence of ancient monasteries. Rubin becomes an alchemist; every ounce of his spirit is in a cosmic dance with the muse he is courting. His focus isn't just intense; it's almost a meditative trance, mirroring the eagle gliding gracefully through the skies, its gaze unshakably rooted on the earth below.

But let's not mistake this for mere focus; this is akin to a sacred communion. Rubin's spirit dives into the essence of the music with the grace of a diver submerging into the enigmatic depths of an ocean, leaving the trivialities of the surface far behind. In this abyss, he uncovers not just notes but the very soul of the symphony.

Consider the poetic alliance between Rick Rubin and the Red Hot Chili Peppers during the genesis of their seminal album. This was not a routine recording; this was a pilgrimage. Rubin transformed an opulent mansion into a sanctuary of creation, a space where the band could be in a relentless embrace with their artistry.

Here, single-tasking was no concept; it was a living, breathing entity. An entity that slept, woke, and breathed music. This unyielding dedication birthed an album that would etch itself into the cultural DNA of an era. It was monumental, and it was not the offspring of a scattered mind.

Rick Rubin's odyssey whispers to our spirits that when you pour your essence into a solitary task, you are not just completing a task – you are painting on the canvas of eternity. Your brain is not a puzzle with missing pieces; it's an orchestra playing a symphony that will resonate through the ages.

Your aspiration might not be to craft a musical masterpiece, but Rubin's path can be threaded regardless of your field. Envision cradling your task in an embrace so intimate that all else fades away. Whether it's sculpting words on a page as an author, illuminating pixels as a graphic designer, or weaving communities as a social worker, your artistry demands the undivided attention of your spirit.

But how you may wonder, can you weave this symphony in a world that is incessantly clamoring for your attention?

Craft Your Fortress of Solitude: Hold on, there's no need to don a cape and take flight like Superman. What you can do is carve out your personal space for focus and tranquility. This could be a serene room at home, a corner in the library, or that cozy spot in a cafe that resonates with your soul. Remember Rick Rubin and the Red Hot Chili Peppers? Think of your space as the creative cocoon that nourishes your focus.

To-Do List Makeover: Often, our to-do lists are like an overflowing buffet - too much to digest. Try to simplify it. Choose your 'big three' for the day – three tasks that you want to give your all. This narrows your focus, and like a sharpshooter, you know what your targets are.

Block Scheduling: Imagine your day as a canvas, and you're the artist. Divide this canvas into blocks, where each block is dedicated to one specific task or project. Just like building a Lego castle, one block at a time, your day takes shape as a work of art.

The 'No' Power: Picture yourself as the sentinel standing guard at the gates of a castle – your castle of concentration. The drawbridge is up, and you determine what gets through. Saying "no" is not a refusal for the sake of being difficult; it's the discerning choice to protect the sanctity of your focus. Like the caretaker of a tranquil garden, you prevent the weeds of distraction from taking root.

Tech Detox: In the bustling digital marketplace, notifications and messages are the street hawkers constantly calling for your attention. Give yourself the gift of specific timeslots for engaging with emails and social media. Let them not be your constant companions, but scheduled appointments. This detachment is like unplugging from the cacophony to embrace the symphony of focus.

The "Two-Minute" Rule: Envision your mind-space as a room. If a task is a small clutter that can be cleared in two minutes, tackle it immediately. It's akin to swatting away a pesky fly that buzzes around incessantly. By doing so, you ensure that your room is decluttered and spacious, ready to host grander pursuits with grace and poise.

Daily Reflection: As dusk settles and the day winds down, gift yourself a moment of reflection. Assess the tapestry of your day. What threads were woven with focus and which got tangled? This reflection is like a gardener inspecting the plants, understanding which ones thrived and where more care is needed.

Find Micro-Moments of Mindfulness: You don't always need a 30-minute meditation session to practice mindfulness. Finding small pockets of time throughout the day to tune in to the present moment can be just as effective.

For instance, while waiting in line at the coffee shop, instead of instinctively reaching for your phone, take a deep breath and observe the sounds and smells around you. You can also use mundane activities such as washing dishes or walking to the mailbox as opportunities to practice mindfulness. These micro-moments can be thought of as 'mental push-ups' that strengthen your mindfulness muscles over time.

And now your workspace, wherever it may be – a quiet nook at home, a bustling office, or your favorite coffee shop – transforms into a haven of focus and productivity. It's a stronghold, fortified not by walls but by the mental barriers you've built against the ceaseless chatter of the outside world. You are in the zone, your every sense honed and aligned with the task at hand. The background noise, the ringing phones, the ping of notifications – they become but a faint hum in the distance.

In this state of mind, you're not just working; you are wielding the powers of single-tasking like a maestro commanding his orchestra. You've left the juggling act behind and embraced the might of focused attention.

Mindfulness is the rudder of this ship you captain. It guides you through the stormy seas of distraction, anchoring you in the present. The waves may crash and the winds may howl, but your ship sails steady.

And in this harmony, something extraordinary unfolds. Your productivity doesn't just increase; it soars. Your creativity doesn't just flow; it cascades. What you create in this sanctuary of focus is no longer mere work – it's a symphony, a tapestry, a sculpture. It's the expression of your finest self.

Chapter 9

Fear of Conflict – The Great Indian Debate

In the late 1970s, a technological revolution was brewing in the garages and workshops of young visionaries. Two of these visionaries, Steve Jobs and Bill Gates, would soon emerge as pioneers in the personal computer industry. Their rivalry, often intense and public, is where we anchor the beginning of our journey into understanding the importance of constructive conflict.

Imagine a young Steve Jobs unveiling the Apple Macintosh in 1984. There is electricity in the air. The Macintosh, with its graphical user interface, is a marvel. In parallel, a young Bill Gates, co-founder of Microsoft, is navigating a different trajectory with MS-DOS and eventually Windows.

The early days of their rivalry were tinged with bitterness. Jobs accused Microsoft of copying the Mac's graphical interface, while Gates argued that Apple couldn't lay claim to the idea either. Their conflict was akin to two tech titans jousting with lightning bolts. This stage of their rivalry embodied the destructive face of conflict - where each party is so engrossed in proving themselves right that there's hardly any room for compromise or collaboration.

However, as the years rolled on, something changed.

As the dust settled, both Jobs and Gates began to recognize that their rivalry could be a source of mutual growth. They each had something the other could benefit from. For Jobs, it was the realization that Microsoft's software could play a key role in revitalizing Apple, which was struggling in the mid-90s. For Gates, it was the understanding that supporting Apple would create a more balanced market, where innovation thrived.

In 1997, in what many would consider a historic moment, Microsoft invested in Apple, and the two companies agreed to share patents. The two giants once engaged in a bitter feud, chose to harness the power of constructive conflict.

Picture two rivers converging into a mightier force. They retain their distinct origins but create something more powerful together. Jobs and Gates began to challenge each other, but this time it was a fertile and creative challenge. They were like two composers from different genres collaborating to create a symphony that neither could have crafted alone.

Real-world innovations, such as the development of the iPod and the evolution of Windows, can trace their lineage to this culture of constructive conflict. The key was that both Jobs and Gates were open to learning, adapting, and growing.

Having witnessed the metamorphosis of rivalry into a collaboration between Steve Jobs and Bill Gates, we now navigate toward the pivotal role of communication in constructive conflict. The crossing of swords between Jobs and Gates led to innovation, but only when they honed the art of communication.

Think of communication as a bridge. When built with care, it connects two seemingly disparate islands. When neglected, it turns into a treacherous crossing.

In the case of Jobs and Gates, the initial communication was more akin to hurling stones across a ravine. For example, Jobs' now-famous outburst, "You're ripping us off!", during an early confrontation with Gates. However, over time, this evolved into a more mature, reciprocal exchange.

Effective communication in conflict is akin to a finely prepared dish; it requires several key ingredients. First, there is active listening - the capacity to truly absorb what the other party is saying without immediately jumping to judgment or formulating a response.

Jobs admitted that the early years of his career were marked by brashness. It wasn't until later that he cultivated the art of listening - a transformation that played a key role in paving the way for his eventual collaboration with Gates.

Second, there's empathy – understanding the perspective and emotions of the other party. For Gates, this meant recognizing the challenges faced by Apple and the potential mutual benefits of a more cooperative relationship.

Lastly, there's articulation – expressing one's perspectives and feelings without aggression or defensiveness. This is where assertiveness plays its part, enabling one to put forth their thoughts firmly but respectfully.

The Gates-Jobs Model – A Template for Professional Growth

Gates and Jobs, through their journey, inadvertently laid out a template for transforming conflict into a catalyst for professional growth.

Imagine you are part of a team working on a high-stakes project. Differences of opinion are bound to arise. Employing the Gates-Jobs model, begin by really listening to what your colleagues have to say. Try to understand not just the words but the concerns, aspirations, and motivations behind them. This active listening becomes the foundation upon which the bridge of communication rests.

Next, apply empathy. Step into the shoes of your teammates. This is not about conceding your stance, but about broadening your perspective.

Finally, articulate your viewpoint with clarity and respect. Find the common ground, and remember that, much like Gates and Jobs, the collective intelligence and creativity of the team are magnified when harnessed constructively.

Their story teaches us that when the seeds of effective communication are sown in the soil of conflict, what emerges is a tree that bears the fruits of innovation, collaboration, and growth.

As our ship sails from the western shores of Gates-Jobs rivalry, we now dock at the vibrant coasts of India, where the dynamics of conflict are woven into an intricate tapestry of culture, tradition, and values. We shall embark on a journey to decode the cultural norms surrounding the conflict in India and decipher how the elements of effective communication can be adapted within this context.

One of the striking facets of the Indian cultural milieu is the emphasis on respect and hierarchy. In Indian society, challenging an authority figure or a senior is often seen as a sign of disrespect. This norm extends into the professional arena as well.

Imagine a young Indian software engineer, Sanjana, brimming with innovative ideas, but holding back from expressing her thoughts in a meeting led by a senior manager. This hesitation stems from the cultural conditioning that promotes deference to authority.

In such a setting, adapting the Jobs-Gates communication model requires a delicate balance. Sanjana might consider expressing her ideas in a manner that acknowledges the experience and authority of the senior, while also diplomatically introducing a different perspective.

Indian culture often values harmony and consensus over confrontation. There is a tendency to avoid conflict to maintain peace, even if it means not addressing critical issues.

Let's consider an example where a team in an Indian company faces internal conflicts. The cultural predisposition might lean towards keeping the discord under wraps rather than addressing it openly, as doing so might be perceived as causing discord or 'rocking the boat'.

However, as we have seen in the case of Jobs and Gates, constructive conflict can be a breeding ground for innovation. In such scenarios, it's important to create a safe space where team members can express their concerns and disagreements openly, but constructively, with an emphasis on problem-solving rather than personal attacks.

In the Indian context, communication, especially in conflict, is often indirect. Rather than straightforward expressions, people tend to communicate through hints or implications.

This subtlety calls for astuteness in understanding and employing indirect modes of communication. In cases where confrontation might be considered abrasive, the art of subtlety and implication can be harnessed for constructive dialogue.

For example, instead of directly stating that a colleague's approach to a problem is flawed, one might suggest exploring 'additional perspectives' or 'alternative routes' to enrich the solution.

As we unravel the cultural threads that define conflict in India, it is evident that navigating conflict in this diverse land is an art in itself. Drawing inspiration from global icons like Jobs and Gates, and adapting their communication principles to the cultural canvas of India, can empower individuals to turn the tides of conflict into a symphony of growth and collaboration.

Navigating conflict within the rich tapestry of Indian cultural norms necessitates more than just a surface-level understanding; it demands a deep dive into strategies that marry the universal principles of communication with the nuances of Indian ethos. Let's unfurl the sails and venture into this riveting journey, equipped with actionable tactics and illuminated by real-life examples and historical insights.

The Wisdom of Socratic Dialogue: The Art of Inquisitive Engagement

Socrates, the ancient Greek philosopher, was renowned for his skill in engaging in meaningful dialogues through a series of thought-provoking questions. This technique, known as the Socratic Method, is about stimulating critical thinking and illuminating ideas, rather than confrontation.

Now, let's transition to contemporary India, where confrontation can be frowned upon, particularly in hierarchical settings. Adopting a Socratic approach by asking questions can be a remarkably potent tool. By engaging in inquiries, individuals can foster dialogue without appearing aggressive.

One of the modern-day personalities who subtly employs this approach is Sundar Pichai, the CEO of Alphabet Inc. He is known for his calm demeanor and analytical mind that often makes use of incisive questions to steer conversations. For Gen Z Indians aspiring to make their mark in the global arena, Pichai's approach can serve as a guide.

Embracing 'Vivad se Samvad': From Debate to Dialogue

Debates have been an integral part of Indian tradition, but in a modern context, transitioning from just debate to dialogue is vital. This means viewing conflicts not as adversarial confrontations but as opportunities for collective problem-solving.

For instance, corporate giants like Tata Group have been known to foster environments where internal dialogue is encouraged. In educational institutions, too, the culture of discussion circles, akin to ancient Indian 'Chaupal' systems, can be integrated.

The Feedback Sandwich: Garnishing Criticism with Positivity

The Indian culture is often characterized by respect, especially towards authority figures. Employing the 'feedback sandwich' technique can prove to be highly effective in such a context. By embedding critical feedback between two positive statements, the critique is more likely to be received constructively.

For example, a young entrepreneur could express their point to a seasoned investor by saying, "Your insights into the market trends are incredibly astute. I think there's potential to further diversify investment portfolios to include emerging technologies. Your guidance could be revolutionary in shaping the market dynamics."

Anonymity as a Beacon of Free Expression

In an atmosphere where individuals might hesitate to voice their concerns openly, leveraging technology for anonymity can be crucial. Modern companies, like Zomato in India, have used anonymous feedback platforms allowing employees to express their concerns and ideas without fear.

The River of Collective Wisdom: Confluence of Ideas

Indian society, with its emphasis on community, offers a unique advantage: the power of collective wisdom. Establishing forums where ideas are not just shared, but woven together, can lead to robust solutions that have communal buy-in.

By integrating these strategies with a discerning understanding of the cultural landscape, professionals in India can transform the currents of conflict into a harmonious flow of creativity and collaboration. The confluence of Socratic wisdom, constructive communication, and cultural sensitivity can form the bedrock upon which the edifice of a new age of conflict navigation is built, resonating with the diverse and rich heritage of India.

Navigating through the maze of cultural sensibilities in India is akin to traversing through the pages of a rich, varied, and sometimes enigmatic chronicle. The communication styles, idioms, and cultural references can vary widely even within short geographical spans. Here, the power of context becomes the north star that guides the ship through these waters.

The Indirect Approach: Decoding the Underlying Messages

One of the fascinating aspects of communication within the Indian context is the prevalence of indirect communication. While in the West, 'yes' generally means affirmative and 'no' negative, in India, the waters are murkier. A nod might not always signify agreement but could be a polite acknowledgment. It is here that understanding the context, non-verbal cues and cultural idiosyncrasies become pivotal. When engaging in conflict resolution, reading between the lines and interpreting the underlying sentiments is essential.

Polychronic Time Perception: Patience is Virtue

In contrast to the monochronic time orientation prevalent in the West, where punctuality and schedules are sacred, India operates on a polychronic perception where multiple tasks often converge and timelines are fluid. Understanding this distinction is critical in conflict resolution. Be prepared for negotiations and discussions to take longer than anticipated, and recognize that this is not necessarily a sign of disinterest or disrespect but rather a cultural difference in time perception.

The Hierarchical Waltz: Navigating the Steps with Grace

India's societal fabric is deeply rooted in hierarchies, be it based on age, position, or social status. When communicating, especially in conflict resolution, being cognizant of these hierarchies and adapting one's communication style accordingly is paramount. Using honorifics, speaking respectfully to elders, and sometimes letting the senior person take the lead in discussions can be integral to successful conflict resolution.

A Tapestry of Languages: The Linguistic Element

The linguistic diversity in India is staggering. While English is widely used in business and education, many people are more comfortable in their native languages. Being attuned to this, and whenever possible, incorporating the local language or dialect can build bridges and facilitate smoother communication.

Symbolism and Cultural References: Engaging with Cultural Intelligence

Indian culture is replete with symbols, idioms, and cultural references. Using these wisely can resonate deeply with an Indian audience. For example, invoking a universally respected figure like Mahatma Gandhi and his principles of non-violence and truth can be very effective in conflict resolution discussions.

Consensus Building: The Indian Tradition of Collective Decision Making

The Indian approach often involves inclusive decision-making. Drawing everyone into the dialogue and striving for consensus, rather than imposing a decision, can often lead to more sustainable resolutions to conflicts.

By harmonizing these elements – decoding indirect communication, respecting hierarchical structures, understanding the fluidity of time, employing linguistic finesse, and engaging with cultural intelligence – one can effectively tailor conflict resolution strategies to resonate with the rich and varied sensibilities of the Indian milieu.

As we glide through the rich tapestry of Indian work culture, think of communication as traditional Indian dance. The grace with which a dancer moves, acknowledging the beat, and the space, reflects how we can navigate the intricate maze of hierarchies and boundaries in Indian workspaces.

Picture this: An Indian family gathering. The patriarchs and matriarchs were seated like royalty. The youngsters gingerly approached them - respect and a hint of trepidation in their eyes. Now, transpose this setting to an Indian office. Not much changes, right? The senior members command respect and often hold the final word, much like the heads of a family. This is where we tread lightly like a dancer ensuring not to step on anyone's toes.

However, there's a twist in our dance. As we embrace globalization, our traditional thumkas need to groove with modern beats. How can we make this fusion dance something to behold?

Picture a mentorship program - a sort of guru-shishya tradition adapted to the corporate stage. Senior members take young protégés under their wings. The dialogue flows but within a cocoon of traditional respect.

Imagine, too, town hall meetings – think of them as the community gatherings of yore, but with PowerPoint presentations. Everyone's invited, and everyone's thoughts matter. The flavor is contemporary, but the aroma is undeniably traditional.

You see, the path winds through the beautiful garden of Indian tradition, without ignoring the vistas of modernity that lie beyond. We're crafting an art form where we don't have to choose between holding on to our roots and branching out.

In essence, we're creating a space where ideas, like rivers, converge. In this confluence, conflicts can find resolutions, ideas can bloom, and the dance can go on – graceful, respectful, and vibrant.

Imagine being an alchemist, not of metals, but of ideas and communications. You stand before your cauldron, the Indian milieu, stirring in ingredients that bring both the age-old wisdom and the zing of modernity to a simmer.

First, let's talk about how we can marry the traditional with the modern in conflict resolution. Picture a weaver interlacing threads to create a fabric. Similarly, you weave the values of respect, empathy, and humility passed down through generations with the modern threads of assertiveness, open communication, and innovation. The result is a fabric strong enough to wrap conflicts without tearing at the seams.

For instance, consider approaching a senior colleague not as a rebel with a cause but as an earnest seeker of knowledge. You say, "I am so impressed by how you handled that project. Can you help me understand the thought process? I have some ideas I would love to discuss with you." Notice how the old-world charm of respect makes room for the freshness of new ideas.

Conflicts, with their roaring intensity, can weigh heavily on our emotions. It's crucial to have resilience at the core of our being, acting as a solid foundation upon which we can stand firm. Here's your guide to building resilience and managing the emotional side of conflicts without wavering.

Be Adaptable Yet Steadfast

Like the versatile bamboo, be adaptable in your responses. Maintain your principles but be open to change in your approach. This involves knowing when to stand firm and when to compromise for the greater good. Adaptability breeds creative solutions.

Engage in Mindful Presence

During a conflict, it's vital to stay fully engaged in the present moment. This means listening actively, not just preparing your rebuttal. Mindfulness helps you to understand the crux of the issue and address it effectively. Develop a mental pause button, so before any reaction, you give yourself the time to choose the most constructive response.

Harness Emotional Intelligence

Being aware of your emotions and those of others is key. Label your emotions accurately and understand their source. This clarity prevents misunderstandings and makes sure that the real issues are what's being discussed, not just emotional reactions.

Empathy as a Bridge

Build bridges with empathy. Understanding and sharing the feelings of others make you human and approachable. It also helps you gauge the deeper issues that the other party might not be able to articulate. You are creating a safe space for open discussion when empathy is in play.

The Power of Breath

Never underestimate the simplicity and effectiveness of taking deep breaths. This is especially important during heated moments. It's not just a stress reliever; it's a clarity-bringer. Your brain functions better with the extra oxygen, and your thoughts will be more coherent.

Adopt a Growth Mindset

See each conflict not as a battle to be won but as a learning experience. Be a student of life, eager to learn and grow. After the conflict, take time to reflect on what happened, what you learned, and how you can improve. This is how personal and professional growth happens – not by winning arguments, but by learning from them.

Developing Solution-Focused Thinking

Keep your eyes on the prize - resolution. Be a problem-solver who is focused on finding solutions rather than dwelling on the issues or laying blame. This proactive approach is contagious and can often inspire others to follow suit.

In the ever-changing landscape of conflict resolution, embracing the essence of continuous learning and adaptation is akin to forging a shield of wisdom. It's important to recognize that the world doesn't stand still and that the complexities of communication and culture are constantly evolving. With this understanding, you should take proactive steps to grow alongside these changes.

After engaging in conflict or a heated discussion, it's essential to hit the pause button and reflect. Analyze the conversations, the reactions, and the resolutions. What could have been handled better? What worked? Reflection is not just an act but a tool that helps carve a more enlightened path.

Of course, no one is perfect, and mistakes are part of the human experience. But within each mistake lies a seed of wisdom. If an email gets misinterpreted or a conversation veers off course, rather than lingering on the mistake, it's imperative to understand the root cause and use this insight for future communications.

In this fast-paced world, it's vital to have your finger on the pulse of change, especially when it comes to diversity and communication. Soaking up new information, engaging in meaningful dialogues, and exposing yourself to a variety of perspectives can bolster your understanding of the cultural tapestry that surrounds you.

Adaptability is an unsung hero in conflict resolution. Being able to tailor your approach, step into another person's shoes, and sometimes even unlearn to relearn can be a game-changer. It's about understanding that the cup of knowledge is never full – there is always room for more.

Realize that resolving conflict isn't about declaring a winner or reaching a finish line. It's about orchestrating a balance, a harmony that respects and acknowledges the spectrum of opinions, emotions, and values at play.

Continuous improvement is the beacon that guides this journey. Like a sculptor chipping away, refining, and polishing, never rest on your laurels. Each conversation, each conflict, and each resolution is a stepping stone in the personal odyssey of development.

As you stride through this unending journey, know that each day, every interaction is an opportunity to learn, adapt, and cultivate an environment of respect and understanding. Through diligence and an open heart, the art of engaging in constructive conflict can become a cornerstone of both personal and professional success.

Chapter 10

Comfort Zone – Breaking Free from the Cocoon

As the dawn breaks, imagine a bird in a nest, high up in a sturdy tree. The nest is warm, and snug, and has a vantage point that shields the bird from predators. This nest, built with meticulous care, is its refuge, its comfort zone. But what if the bird never leaves the nest? It will never soar through the skies, never feel the rush of the wind beneath its wings, and never experience the sheer freedom that is its birthright. Like this bird, humans too have their nests - zones of comfort that keep them safe but can also keep them ensnared.

The concept of the comfort zone is often discussed with ambivalence. Is it a haven that brings peace and stability, or is it more akin to a gilded cage, splendid but confining? It's like being in a cozy room with a blazing fireplace in the winter - it's warm and comfortable inside, but if you never step outside, you will never experience the snow's crisp freshness or the thrill of making the first footprints on a snowy path. Comfort zones are not inherently bad. They provide a mental state of ease and familiarity where our stress and anxiety levels are low.

However, they can be double-edged swords. Staying within the confines of what's familiar and comfortable for too long can create barriers to learning, innovation, and fulfilling one's potential.

Moving to the streets and homes of India, the comfort zone takes on additional layers. In India, where family ties are strong and traditions run deep, the comfort zone is often woven into the very fabric of one's identity. Here, the community is interwoven with the self. Decisions, ambitions, and life choices are often influenced, if not dictated, by family expectations, societal norms, and cultural traditions.

Imagine a young lady in a small town in India, brilliant and creative, who dreams of becoming a fashion designer. However, her family's expectations are for her to become an engineer or a doctor, as those professions have long been revered in her community. Her comfort zone, and by extension, her family's comfort zone, dictates the familiar path - the path trodden by many before her. To break away from this path and pursue her dreams, she would have to step outside her comfort zone and face the unknown. In doing so, she would not only be challenging her fears and insecurities but also the expectations and norms of her family and community.

The Indian context adds a rich tapestry of culture, tradition, and societal expectations to the concept of the comfort zone. It's not just about an individual's fears and insecurities; it's about a collective comfort zone that has been built over generations.

In a lush garden, the roses stand tall, their petals a symphony of colors. Tourists and locals alike often walk past these roses, pausing to inhale their intoxicating scent. What they often don't see are the thorns that lie hidden amongst the blossoms. Much like these roses, the comfort zone, too, has its hidden thorns.

In the comforting embrace of familiarity, it's easy to become complacent. After all, why venture into the unknown when the known is so comforting? The first thorn in the comfort zone is complacency, and it's a particularly insidious one. Complacency is like a slow-acting poison; it seeps into your life quietly, often without you even noticing it. Before you know it, you are trapped.

In the professional sphere, complacency can be career-limiting. Imagine a talented software engineer with a flair for coding. He's content in his current role, and the thought of taking on a new project or learning a new coding language seems unnecessary. As he remains nestled in his comfort zone, the world around him evolves. New programming languages emerge, and new methodologies are developed. Over time, his skills become outdated. Had he ventured out of his comfort zone and continuously evolved his skill set, he might have climbed the ladder or even made groundbreaking innovations.

In personal life, complacency can manifest as a stagnation of personal growth and development. Take, for example, someone who loves to play the guitar but never pushes themselves to learn new techniques or explore different genres. While they may find solace in playing the same tunes, they miss out on the joy of discovering new sounds and the sense of achievement that comes with mastering a challenging piece.

Complacency and stagnation are not just individual issues; they have societal implications as well. When communities or even entire nations become entrenched in their collective comfort zones, the results can be stifling.

In the context of India, the weight of tradition can sometimes act as an anchor, holding back the tides of progress. For instance, traditional gender roles can create a societal comfort zone where men are expected to be breadwinners and women homemakers. This not only limits the aspirations and potential of countless women but also deprives society of diverse talents and perspectives.

Now, let's spread our wings to find the antidote to these thorns.

Take a deep breath and prepare for a thrilling journey into the cradle of your thoughts, emotions, and creativity – the human brain. Picture it - a densely tangled network, shimmering with electrical impulses and pulsating with life. This miraculous organ, roughly the size of two clenched fists, holds about 86 billion neurons connected through trillions of synapses. Just take a moment to let the magnitude of that sink in!

Now, imagine the brain as an endless labyrinth, where each pathway and chamber represents different skills, memories, and experiences. When you live within your comfort zone, you mostly traverse the same familiar paths. It's cozy and secure, but it doesn't push the boundaries of the labyrinth.

This is where the magic of neuroplasticity comes into play. Neuroplasticity is like the brain's own wizardry, which allows it to morph and adapt. When you challenge yourself with a novel experience or skill, your brain acts like an intrepid adventurer, forging new pathways and building bridges between chambers in the labyrinth.

These fresh connections make your brain more versatile and agile.

For instance, let's say you decide to learn a new language. As you grapple with alien sounds and syntax, your brain constructs new neural networks to handle the linguistic complexity. Not only does this enhance your language skills, but it also boosts your memory and attention span. It's like adding an extension to your brain's mansion, complete with state-of-the-art facilities!

Moreover, the brain has a fascinating link with your emotions. As you challenge yourself and achieve milestones, your brain releases chemicals like dopamine and serotonin, which are often referred to as "feel-good" hormones. This is why, when you conquer a fear or solve a complex problem, you feel a wave of euphoria and accomplishment. It's the brain's way of giving you a standing ovation for your performance!

By consistently embracing challenges and venturing beyond the familiar terrains of your brain's labyrinth, you not only build a more robust and adaptable mind but also fortify your self-esteem and self-efficacy. It's akin to being both the architect and the resident of an ever-expanding, luxurious mental landscape.

So, equip yourself with the torch of curiosity and the compass of determination, and set forth to explore the uncharted territories of your cerebral wonderland. Each step you take outside your comfort zone is a step towards crafting a more enriched, fulfilled, and empowering life.

As you stand on the precipice of new experiences, your mind as eager as an explorer, it is imperative that you carry the right tools. In the realm of personal growth, skill-building, and continuous learning are akin to a well-stocked traveler's backpack.

Let's paint a picture: A young Indian entrepreneur, with stars in her eyes and an unyielding resolve, dreams of carving a niche in the tech world with her startup. While her computer science degree has endowed her with coding expertise, she recognizes that to navigate the choppy waters of entrepreneurship, she needs more than just technical skills. It's like setting sail on the vast ocean; a sailor needs to know not just how to hoist the sails, but also how to read the weather, chart a course, and negotiate with traders.

With this wisdom, she plunges into a whirlwind of learning. Business management courses become her cartography lessons, teaching her how to chart her company's course. Marketing seminars become her navigation, guiding her through the currents of consumer interests. Each networking event is akin to sharing tales and maps with fellow voyagers, amassing a treasure trove of insights. Every financial management lesson strengthens the hull of her ship, ensuring it can weather storms.

But there's more to continuous learning than the structured realm of courses and seminars. It's an all-encompassing embrace of knowledge that can be found in the pages of a book, the verses of a poem, or the casual wisdom imparted through conversations. It's akin to picking up seashells of wisdom along the shore, each unique and valuable.

This insatiable curiosity leads our entrepreneur to voraciously read books, not just on business, but on history, culture, and philosophy. She engages in spirited discussions with people from diverse backgrounds, each conversation adding layers to her understanding of the world.

And lo and behold, these assorted skills and eclectic knowledge converge, giving her a kaleidoscopic lens through which to view her venture. Her tech startup, fueled by a symphony of skills, thrives and evolves into a beacon of innovation.

Just as our entrepreneur built her arsenal of skills, so can you. Enrich your mind, weave together the threads of different disciplines, and chart your extraordinary journey.

Change is like walking through an unknown territory, and having a support system is like having a trusty compass and a guide by your side. Peer support – the encouragement and backing from friends, family, and like-minded individuals – can often be the secret ingredient in propelling you forward in your journey.

Let's talk about someone who is trying to chart a unique career path that isn't the norm in their community. The skepticism from around can be quite the hurdle. But, when this person finds friends or a group who understand and support their aspirations, it's like fuel to their fire. That validation and motivation can sometimes be all that's needed to turn dreams into reality.

But wait, peer support isn't just an emotional pep squad. It's also an incredible resource pool. Think about it – a diverse group of people bringing different skills and knowledge to the table. It's like having a library with a human touch. Need to learn how to create a business plan? Someone in your support circle might have a template. Looking for feedback on your website design? There's probably someone who can help.

And let's not overlook the diversity in a peer group. Each individual is like a book with different chapters and lessons. The artist might teach you to see the world in a different hue, the technologist might show you how to streamline your work, and the philosopher might help you find balance. Each perspective adds a new layer to your personal and professional growth.

It's crucial to remember that peer support is not a one-way street. It's an exchange - sometimes you're the giver, sometimes you're the receiver. This reciprocity is what keeps the circle alive and thriving.

Additionally, don't hesitate to look beyond your immediate circle when needed. Sometimes, the best support can come from unexpected places or the wisdom of experts in your field of interest. Keep your antennas up!

In essence, a strong peer support system is like having an arsenal of tools, a treasure trove of wisdom, and a cheering squad, all rolled into one. It is the nudge when you hesitate, the pat on the back when you succeed, and the arms that pick you up when you fall. Cultivate it, cherish it, and be an active participant. Through the synergy of collaboration, the path of change becomes a shared journey of triumphs.

Let's now embark on the inspiring journey of Neysa Sanghavi, a young Indian woman who ventured far beyond her comfort zone to build bridges between cultures.

Neysa, who hails from Udaipur, always had an inquisitive mind and a yearning to explore the world. Her journey began when she took the plunge to study abroad. She opted for a destination that many might not consider – Rwanda, a country in East Africa. This choice was unconventional; Rwanda has been through tumultuous times, and there was little familiarity with its culture. But Neysa's adventurous spirit knew no bounds.

As she landed in Rwanda for her college education, she realized that many Rwandans were unfamiliar with India and its rich heritage. At the same time, Neysa found that people back home in India had little knowledge about Rwanda. This was a golden opportunity – a call to break free from the comfortable shell of being just a student.

With her heart set on fostering connections between India and Rwanda, Neysa embarked on a mission. She interacted with the local communities, learned Kinyarwanda (the local language), and started promoting Rwandan culture in India and Indian culture in Rwanda through various platforms.

But what makes her story remarkable is not just her determination but her ability to turn this passion into a recognized initiative. The Rwandan Government, seeing her sincere dedication, officially appointed her as the Brand Ambassador of Rwanda to India when she was just 21.

Neysa's journey is a testament to how stepping out of one's comfort zone can not only lead to personal growth but can also create ripples of positive change in the world. Through her intercultural exchange, she has built bridges of understanding, goodwill, and friendship between the two nations.

What Neysa has shown us is that your comfort zone is not just a physical space – it's a mental and emotional space too. By embracing the unknown and actively engaging with it, one can turn into a catalyst for change and growth. This is particularly powerful in the present globalized world, where cross-cultural understanding can be a potent tool for peace and development.

Neysa Sanghavi's story encourages young minds to look beyond the obvious, harness the power of curiosity, and not be afraid to chart unknown territories. In this journey, every interaction can be a learning experience, and every small effort can contribute to a larger purpose.

As we marvel at the bridge-building endeavors of Neysa, let's now navigate the digital waves with Advait Thakur, who plunged into the ocean of technology entrepreneurship at an astonishingly tender age.

In the digital age, where technology is the driving force behind the transformation, Advait Thakur exemplifies what can be achieved when a young mind refuses to be bound by the conventional timelines of success. Born in Mumbai, Advait had a fascination with computers that was apparent from a very young age. While most kids of his age were busy playing games or struggling with homework, Advait's thirst for knowledge led him down a different path.

At the age of 15, when most teenagers are just coming to grips with high school, Advait took a leap that would set him apart. He founded Apex Infosys India, a technology company focused on web development, app development, and digital marketing. This was not a casual endeavor; his company swiftly garnered attention for its innovative solutions and quality services.

It's crucial to realize the audacity of this move. Being a young entrepreneur, especially in a field as competitive and rapidly evolving as technology, could have been overwhelming. But Advait's clarity of purpose and dedication enabled him to turn challenges into opportunities. His ability to adapt, learn, and implement was the wind beneath his wings.

In the years following the inception of Apex Infosys India, Advait's name began to resonate not just within India but globally. His achievements started stacking up, including being recognized by Google and receiving accolades for being one of the youngest entrepreneurs in the tech industry.

What's inspiring about Advait Thakur's story is the reminder that age is no barrier to achievement. His journey tells us that, sometimes, stepping out of the comfort zone means not waiting for the "right time." Instead, it's about embracing the present, wielding the baton of passion, and orchestrating a symphony of innovation.

Just as Neysa bridged cultures, Advait is bridging gaps in the digital world, bringing innovative solutions to the global market. His story exemplifies how stepping out of the comfort zone in pursuit of passion can not only bring personal success but also contribute to the larger technological and entrepreneurial landscape.

Both Neysa and Advait's tales are a clarion call to the youth – the world is a canvas, and you hold the paintbrush. Don't hesitate to paint your path, even if the colors you choose are different from what's traditionally expected. The masterpieces of change and innovation await the daring strokes of those willing to step beyond their comfort zones.

As we have traversed the inspiring tales of Neysa Sanghavi and Advait Thakur, it's time to turn the spotlight inward and ask, "How can I carve my path beyond my comfort zone?"

One of the most crucial elements in this voyage is setting and pursuing personal goals. Much like a sailor charting a course across the open seas, personal goals serve as your North Star, guiding you through the vast ocean of possibilities.

Setting personal goals begins with self-reflection. It's essential to introspect and identify what you want to achieve in different facets of your life – be it your career, personal development, relationships, or hobbies. However, these goals mustn't be set in stone. Think of them as a pencil sketch rather than an inked drawing, allowing for adjustments as you grow and evolve.

Now, let's talk about the SMART approach to goal setting: Specific, Measurable, Achievable, Relevant, and Time-bound. This approach ensures that your goals are well-defined and that you can track your progress. It's like installing GPS for your dreams; you've got the destination and the route with all the milestones in place.

Pursuing the goals is where the rubber meets the road. It requires dedication, consistency, and a willingness to face and overcome hurdles. Along the way, don't forget to celebrate the small wins. These are your precious treasures, the winds that fill your sails and propel you further on your journey.

Moreover, surround yourself with a support system - friends, family, mentors, or peers who can offer guidance, encouragement, and even a different perspective when needed. Remember how peer support played an instrumental role for Advait Thakur? Your personal support network can be the crew that helps you steer through stormy waters.

Lastly, embrace the fact that sometimes, despite your best efforts, things may not go as planned. At such times, it's important to be adaptable and resilient. Take a step back, reassess, and if necessary, chart a new course.

By setting and diligently pursuing your personal goals, you're not just stepping out of your comfort zone; you're launching an expedition into uncharted waters, discovering new lands, and growing into a version of yourself that is boundless in its potential.

Failure is like a sudden gust of wind that can knock us off course, or sometimes even capsize our boat. But, what if we could harness that wind? What if we could use the energy of failure to fill our sails and propel us forward? This is where embracing failure and learning from it becomes the keystone in building resilience.

Failure is often cloaked in negative connotations, especially in cultures where success is glorified. However, the most intrepid explorers of human potential understand that failure is not the antithesis of success, but rather its precursor. It's a powerful teacher that reveals the areas where we need to build our skills, re-evaluate our strategies, and deepen our resolve.

Let's take a leaf out of Thomas Edison's book. When he was trying to invent the electric light bulb, it took him over a thousand attempts to find the right filament that wouldn't burn out quickly. He famously said, "I have not failed. I've just found 10,000 ways that won't work." This epitomizes the mindset of embracing failure as a learning process.

Reflecting on the story of Advait Thakur that we discussed earlier in this chapter, one can only imagine the challenges and failures he might have faced on his journey to becoming a young tech entrepreneur. His audacity to persevere through failures and learn from them has played a significant role in shaping his success.

So, how can one develop the ability to embrace failure? First and foremost, it's about shifting our perspective and seeing failure as feedback, not as a personal indictment. It's about asking ourselves, "What can I learn from this experience? How can I improve? What needs to change in my approach?"

Furthermore, sharing our experiences of failure with others can be incredibly empowering. It not only helps in finding support but also in realizing that failure is a universal experience - it's part of the human journey.

Moreover, building resilience is about cultivating emotional intelligence. It's about understanding and managing our emotions when faced with setbacks, and constructively channeling them.

Ultimately, embracing failure and learning from it is like learning to sail against the wind. It requires skill, courage, and adaptability. But once mastered, it allows us to venture into waters and undertake voyages that we previously thought were beyond our reach.

As we steer through the journey of self-growth and exploration, having a guiding star can be invaluable. This is where mentors and role models enter the picture. They are the lighthouses guiding us through tumultuous seas, the compasses that help us stay true to our course.

A mentor, often someone who has sailed the same seas you are venturing into, can provide the wisdom of experience. They can help you anticipate and navigate through obstacles, and they often offer a different perspective that enables you to see things in a new light. Having a mentor is like having an experienced captain on board, one who's already charted the waters and knows how to avoid hidden reefs and treacherous currents.

Role models, on the other hand, serve as a source of inspiration. They are the embodiment of what's possible if one dares to sail beyond the horizon. They don't necessarily need to be personally involved in your journey but can be figures you look up to, whose values, achievements, or qualities resonate with you.

For instance, many young entrepreneurs may look up to figures like Elon Musk or Richard Branson for their audacity and innovation. Similarly, young Indian sportspersons might look up to Virat Kohli or P.V. Sindhu as role models for their dedication and achievements in sports.

It's essential to realize that mentors and role models don't have to be famous or immensely successful. They can be teachers, family members, friends, or colleagues. What's important is the positive influence they exert, guiding you to grow and learn.

Breaking free from the comfort zone is not a one-time event, but a continuous journey of discovery, learning, and growth. It's about shedding the layers that confine us and embracing the endless possibilities that lie in the uncharted skies beyond the cocoon.

The journey might be fraught with risks and failures, but with the right mindset, tools, and guidance, it leads to unimaginable heights. Like a caterpillar metamorphosing into a butterfly, when you step out of your comfort zone, you don't just change; you transform into a more vibrant, resilient, and fulfilled version of yourself.

Embrace your wings. Trust in your capacity to grow, adapt, and soar. Seek out challenges, savor new experiences, and be open to learning. Cultivate resilience, seek wisdom from mentors, and let role models inspire you.

As you set sail on your odyssey beyond your comfort zone, remember that you're not alone. You're part of a vast, interconnected web of dreamers, explorers, and change-makers. Together, through our journeys, we write the collective story of human potential and progress. So, spread your wings, brave dreamer, and take flight into the boundless skies of possibility.

Chapter 11

Redefining Success – The Indian Dream Reimagined

As a civilization that dates back over five millennia, India's rich tapestry is woven with countless threads, each representing a different era, dynasty, or cultural tide. The Indian Dream, as an aspiration representing success and fulfillment, has evolved significantly over time, adapting to the changing contours of history.

In ancient India, during the Vedic period, the concept of success was heavily anchored in the pursuit of the four pillars of life, or Purusharthas: Dharma (righteousness), Artha (wealth), Kama (pleasures), and Moksha (liberation). The attainment of spiritual wisdom and adherence to duty formed the core of one's aspirations.

Fast forward to the days of the Maurya and Gupta empires, where valor and statecraft emerged as defining factors of success. The concept of Chakravartin, or the ideal universal ruler, was celebrated. The vision of success was inseparable from the greatness of rulers who were both mighty and just.

As the pages of history turned to the Mughal era, grandeur, and artistic patronage took center stage.

The Indian Dream was one of splendor, as the Mughal emperors lavished the land with architectural wonders like the Taj Mahal, and a flourishing of arts and culture.

With the advent of the British Raj, Western influences brought about seismic shifts in Indian society. Education, particularly in English and Western sciences, emerged as the gatekeeper to success. It was in this period that the Indian Dream began its tectonic shift towards modernity, where success was gauged by colonial standards – degrees, salaried jobs, and material wealth.

Today, in an independent India caught in the whirlwind of globalization and technological revolution, the Indian Dream is no longer a single-thread narrative. It's a kaleidoscope of ambitions that range from entrepreneurial ventures to social changes, from technological innovations to artistic expressions. The new generation yearns for global recognition, while also seeking a sense of purpose.

The river of legacy that flows through the Indian subcontinent is deep and timeless. Like the mighty Ganges that have nurtured civilizations, this legacy shapes the ethos and aspirations of its people. Stories passed down through generations, myths that have attained the stature of epics, and historical figures who loom larger than life, collectively, they all contribute to the weight of legacy that every Indian carries.

However, this weight can be both empowering and burdensome. It's empowering because it connects individuals to a rich heritage, offering wisdom and identity. But it can also be a burden when the shadows of the past limit the wings of the present. The lives of Rama and Arjuna, the valor of Rani Padmini, the genius of

Aryabhata, and the righteousness of King Harishchandra – these are not just stories but yardsticks against which society often measures success.

In contemporary India, this translates to enormous pressure to uphold family honor, follow traditional career paths, and sometimes suppress individualistic aspirations that don't conform to the societal mold. The modern Indian is often perched on a tightrope, balancing the weight of historical legacy and the pull of personal dreams.

But as the winds of change continue to blow, there is an evident shift in mindset, especially among the younger generation. They are beginning to question, evaluate, and sometimes reinterpret the narratives that have been handed down to them.

The Quintessential Indian Success Story

Diving into the heart of Indian society, one cannot overlook the triad that has historically been revered as the hallmarks of success: wealth, status, and social standing. These have been the cornerstones on which Indian society built its aspirations and dreams. From the lively lanes of Varanasi to the bustling streets of Mumbai, this triad resonates in daily conversations, community gatherings, and family expectations.

Wealth, in particular, has been seen as a fundamental measure of success. In India, with its deeply-rooted history of trade, commerce, and agricultural prosperity, affluence has long been equated with a person's worth. Moreover, with a population exceeding a billion people, the quest for economic security is fierce. It's as if Lakshmi, the goddess of wealth, bestows her blessings on those deemed successful.

Closely intertwined with wealth is the notion of status. A high-status job, particularly in government, medicine, engineering, or law, is often perceived as the golden ticket to respectability. The prefix 'Doctor' or the epithet 'IIT-graduate' opens the floodgates of societal admiration. It's almost as if the battles of Mahabharata are being fought in examination halls and job interviews, and titles are the modern-day equivalent of battle honors.

Social standing is the third pillar. Traditionally, Indian society has been structured around a complex web of castes, clans, and communities. While modern India has made significant strides in shedding the regressive aspects of this social structure, the undercurrents of lineage and familial prestige continue to wield influence. Marriages are still often negotiated like treaties that should bolster the family's social standing. The echoes of royal titles and ancestral heritage still resonate in the hallowed halls of the aristocracy.

As contemporary India embraces globalization, this triad witnesses an interesting metamorphosis. The tech-savvy entrepreneur, the internationally acclaimed artist, or the social activist championing change, are now earning their place among the traditionally revered.

However, with the rapidly changing socio-economic landscape and the exposure to global cultures, there is a brewing restlessness, especially among the younger generation. There is an increasing yearning for something more profound, something that transcends the conventional hallmarks of success.

The echoes of the age-old adage, "Padhoge Likhoge Banoge Nawab" (If you study, you will become a noble), reverberate through the hallways of Indian homes. Education has been the bedrock, the foundation upon which the aspirations of millions are built. The sacrosanctity of education as a key to success is an unspoken truth.

In a traditional Indian household, the trajectory is often preordained: perform exceptionally in school, pursue a degree in a high-paying field, and then land a secure job. It's akin to a well-trodden path in a dense jungle; many have walked it, so it must lead somewhere promising. And there is a sense of comfort in familiarity, even if it doesn't align with one's passions or aptitudes.

Engineering and medicine have often been heralded as the epitome of educational achievement. The neighborhood erupts into celebrations when a teenager cracks the Joint Entrance Exam or secures a seat in a medical college. For many families, this moment is the culmination of not just the student's hard work, but a collective family dream. The financial and emotional investment is often so immense that diverging from this set path is unthinkable.

However, this ironclad route, though gilded with the promise of stability and prosperity, has its shadows. The pressure to conform to societal expectations leads to a stifling environment for creativity and self-exploration. Mental health issues and stress among students are alarming concerns that often get swept under the rug

Now, throw in the ingredients of social constructs. In India, societal validation can sometimes have the gravitational pull of a black hole. The yearning for social standing and the weight of the 'log kya kitenge (what will people say) mentality can heavily influence the life choices individuals make. Be it choosing a career, selecting a life partner, or even buying a house, the ever-present societal gaze can mold and shape the perception of what success should look like.

Yet, as we peel back the layers, it's heartening to see that the new generation is beginning to question these age-old perceptions. Armed with exposure to global cultures and bolstered by the power of social media, young Indians are starting to redefine success on their terms. They're like sculptors, chipping away at the monolith of tradition to craft a more nuanced, inclusive, and personal definition of success.

The interplay between family, religion, and social constructs is akin to a time-honored dance, passed down through generations. However, with each passing day, the steps of this dance are evolving, as the dancers twirl to the beat of a rapidly changing world.

The success stories of unconventional careers are slowly carving alternative paths in that dense jungle. Stand-up comedians, independent musicians, writers, startup enthusiasts - these are no longer characters from a far-off land; they are the next-door neighbors, the cousins, the friends.

Take, for instance, the story of Bhuvan Bam, an Indian YouTube sensation who carved a niche for himself through his channel BB Ki Vines. Bhuvan, a Delhiite, initially started as a singer performing in restaurants. He inadvertently stumbled into the world of YouTube when a news reporter's video he made went viral. His comedic sketches, relatable characters, and the raw appeal of his content created a cult following. Through sheer talent, innovation, and persistence, Bhuvan Bam broke the shackles of the conventional career path and is now a household name, inspiring countless others to follow their dreams.

Furthermore, with the advent of the internet and the ease of access to global platforms, the young generation of India is no longer restricted by geographical limitations. They are global citizens, and their playground is boundless.

So, is the traditional education and career paradigm still the ironclad route to prosperity? Maybe for some. But for an increasing number of young Indians, success is being redefined to encompass a sense of fulfillment, creativity, and impact beyond the conventional metrics.

As we witness the dawn of this new era, it becomes pertinent to recognize and foster an environment that not only respects traditional paths but also celebrates the alternative journeys that paint the multifarious tapestry of modern India.

Amidst the swirling currents of a society that so often dictates the routes to be taken, there are those daring individuals who swim against the tide. These trailblazers, armed with a vision and unyielding tenacity, don't just transform their destinies, but sometimes even alter the collective conscience.

One such standout is Kartiki Gonsalves, whose enthralling documentary, "The Elephant Whisperers," not only brought her acclaim but also earned an Oscar. Born and raised in a small village, Kartiki's thirst for storytelling led her down an unpaved road. Her documentary gave voice to the conservationists dedicated to protecting endangered elephants. Through her lens, she weaves tales that captivate and educate, bringing much-needed attention to crucial issues. This is not the usual path of glory that many treads, but it's one that holds a profound impact and marks her indelible footprint in the sands of time.

Now, cast your gaze upon the remarkable journey of Avani Lekhara, a Paralympian shooter who, despite her physical challenges, has proved that relentless spirit knows no bounds. After a car accident that changed the course of her life, Avani did not wallow in despair; she took up shooting and went on to win a gold medal at the Tokyo Paralympics. She is an epitome of resilience and a shining beacon to countless others.

In the realm of entrepreneurship, Trishneet Arora, the founder of TAC Security, comes to mind. In his early 20s, Trishneet is a cybersecurity whiz who turned his passion into a successful enterprise that protects organizations from data breaches and cyber threats.

He didn't tread the worn path of conventional careers but ventured into an area that is both cutting-edge and essential in the modern digital world. While the trailblazers of Modern India have been scripting their sagas of triumph, they stand on the shoulders of giants who came before them. The annals of history brim with visionaries who, through sheer audacity, reshaped the contours of possibility.

These mavericks, with their unyielding determination, have not just etched their names in the echelons of history but have also left behind a treasure trove of wisdom for the aspirants. So let us dive into the archives and retrieve some of these invaluable pearls, insights from the legends who dared to tread where others wouldn't venture.

Picture a woman in India, her pen poised over paper, not just crafting sentences but challenging the very fabric of society with her words. Arundhati Roy, the author who rose to international acclaim with her novel The God of Small Things, is a paragon of courage and unadulterated artistic expression. For Roy, the pages were not just a canvas but a battleground to wage wars against social injustices.

Her triumph did not lie in the accolades, such as the Man Booker Prize in 1997, but in using her craft to echo the whispers of the marginalized. She is a testament to the power of authentic expression. To those treading the path of art, she exemplifies that true success lies not in the validation of accolades but in the fulfillment of utilizing one's art as a conduit for the deepest convictions and compassion.

Now, let us traverse continents and delve into the buzzing alleys of Silicon Valley. Here, in the sanctum of innovation, a young Steve Jobs, co-founder of Apple, nurtured an insatiable hunger to reshape the world. When Jobs stood before the graduating class of Stanford in 2005, his words were not just an address but a distillation of a life lived on the edge of innovation. His mantra, "Stay hungry, stay foolish," was an anthem for restless souls who yearned to paint the canvas of life with broad strokes of creativity and curiosity.

Steve Jobs didn't just build a company; he sculpted an era. His nonlinear odyssey, punctuated with soaring highs and humbling lows, was a masterclass in unwavering resolve. To the innovators, entrepreneurs, and seekers, his life exemplifies that the crucible of failure is but a forge for greatness, and that contentment is the adversary of innovation.

These luminaries, through their indomitable spirits, have carved pathways through the dense forests of convention. They beckon us to not tread lightly but to make our marks indelible. In the words of Roy, let the ink of conviction flow freely, and as Jobs professed, let the fires of curiosity consume the banal.

So as you, the dreamer and seeker, stand at the precipice of possibilities, remember that your path is yours to forge.

Charting your Odyssey

Consider life as a vast tapestry, where every decision, experience, and belief interweaves to create your unique story. However, often this tapestry is woven in patterns dictated by external influences rather than our inner selves. Reframing your narrative is about taking charge of the threads and weaving a tapestry that reflects your true essence.

Let's start by acknowledging and deconstructing the mental barriers. These barriers often wear masks – they disguise themselves as societal norms, fear of failure, or the daunting weight of expectations. By bringing them into the light, we can see them for what they are: constraints that need not define us. It's like decluttering a room that's been gathering dust for years. As you clean, you realize the space you have to redecorate according to your taste.

Now, turn inward for a deep self-reflection. This is the phase where you have an honest conversation with yourself. What is it that gives you a sense of fulfillment? Is your vision of success genuinely yours, or is it an echo of someone else's voice? Delve into the 'whys' of your desires. Understand that if a goal doesn't align with your core values, achieving it might not bring the contentment you seek.

As you clear the fog of external influences, you might find that the path ahead isn't a straight line but a rich landscape with multiple trails. Here, empower yourself through learning and exposure. Read voraciously, engage with diverse communities, and be open to new experiences. The world is an eclectic mosaic of cultures, ideologies, and possibilities. Every exposure can add a new color to your tapestry.

Remember to exercise patience and compassion toward yourself during this process. Changing a lifetime's worth of mindset and beliefs is not an overnight endeavor. It's a journey, sometimes a winding one.

Now comes the act of weaving your tapestry with intention. With every thread you add, with every pattern you create, be conscious. Know that this is your creation, reflective of your newfound understanding and aspirations.

In reframing your narrative, you're not just altering a story. You're claiming ownership of your life's tapestry, ensuring that every thread resonates with the depths of who you are and what you stand for.

Building your ladder to success is akin to crafting a customized tool that will help you reach the heights you aspire to. However, a ladder built on shaky foundations or with weak rungs can prove to be unreliable or even hazardous. To ensure that your ladder is sturdy and serves its purpose, it's crucial that its construction is aligned with your values and strengths.

First, let's talk about the foundation. A ladder that's anchored in your core values has a strong base. It's imperative to recognize what you stand for. Is it creativity, innovation, family, integrity, or perhaps community service? Whatever your values are, let them be the ground on which you erect your ladder. When your actions and goals are in sync with your values, you're less likely to be swayed by distractions or to build a ladder that leads to someone else's version of success.

Now, for the rungs of the ladder – these represent the goals and milestones. Each rung should be a step that takes you closer to the fulfillment of your aspirations. However, instead of merely setting broad goals, break them down into smaller, more manageable tasks. For instance, if your goal is to write a book, one of the lower rungs could be writing a certain number of words each day.

Next, consider your strengths. Utilize them to your advantage as you build and climb your ladder. Are you a good communicator, a creative thinker, or perhaps you have an eye for detail? Whatever your strengths are, find ways to incorporate them into your goals. For example, if you're a great communicator and your value is community service, one of the rungs could be starting a podcast to raise awareness on social issues.

But, what about your weaknesses? It's important not to ignore them. Being aware of your limitations allows you to either work on them or find alternatives. For instance, if you're not great at time management, you could use apps or tools that help you stay on track.

As you make your ascent, you may realize that some rungs need repositioning or that the ladder itself needs a change in direction. That's okay. Building your ladder is a dynamic process. The market changes, you evolve, and new opportunities arise. Flexibility and adaptability are key.

Lastly, don't forget to celebrate each time you reach a new rung. Acknowledging your achievements, however small, fuels your motivation and reminds you of the progress you've made.

Building your ladder is not just a metaphor for success; it's a living embodiment of your journey, built brick by brick with your values, goals, strengths, and the lessons you learn along the way.

Cultivating a supportive ecosystem is an integral part of forging your path to success. The encouragement, advice, and shared experiences within this network can prove invaluable in overcoming challenges and making critical decisions.

The Wisdom of Mentors

Having mentors is akin to standing on the shoulders of giants. Through their years of experience, they have amassed a wealth of knowledge that can save you from reinventing the wheel. Think of how a young writer would benefit from the guidance of an established author like Arundhati Roy, who we discussed earlier in the chapter. A mentor can help you hone your craft, advise you on navigating the industry, and be your sounding board. Additionally, mentors can open doors by introducing you to their network, which can be priceless in your journey.

The Power of Peer Networks

While mentors offer a bird's eye view, peers provide the camaraderie and empathy of those who are in the trenches with you. These are the fellow warriors who understand the day-to-day challenges because they are living them too. Remember the inspiring tales of individuals like Kartiki Gonsalves, whose documentary won an Oscar? Surround yourself with such ambitious individuals who are also carving their paths. The energy and motivation in such a peer group can be contagious, pushing you to explore your boundaries.

Engaging with Communities

Communities can be the bedrock on which you build your success. These groups – sometimes formal, other times informal – are pools of shared interests, values, or ambitions. They are the places where you can find both mentors and peers. Being an active member of relevant communities can offer you resources, such as workshops or networking events, that are otherwise not easy to find. In a community, you are part of something bigger – a collective force that can be a wind beneath your wings.

Reciprocity in Relationships

As you cultivate these relationships, it's imperative to remember that support is a two-way street. Be open to providing assistance, sharing your insights, and being there for others. Success is not a solo journey, and the goodwill you build by helping others can often return to you manifold in unexpected ways.

As the final brushstrokes touch this tapestry we've woven, we stand back to gaze at the panorama before us. We've traversed through the annals of tradition, danced in the shadows of monoliths, and tasted the nectar of the mavericks' dreams. The Indian Dream, once seen as rigid and unyielding, has the potential to be as varied and vibrant as the nation itself.

It is an opportune moment to realize that success is not an edifice set in stone but rather a mosaic created from the shards of our experiences, values, and aspirations. We don't have to be shackled by the expectations of the old.

Let this not be an end, but rather the heralding of countless beginnings. Your dreams await; let them not be dreams deferred. Through courage, tenacity, and a little audacity, may you paint the stars with your reimagined definition of success.

Chapter 12

FOMO – The Fear of Missing Out on Life

The digital revolution and globalization have transformed the way we interact, learn, and live. We are more connected than ever, yet ironically, many of us grapple with an insidious phenomenon – Fear Of Missing Out, commonly known as FOMO. But before we delve into how FOMO pervades our modern lives, let's trace its origins and evolution in human behavior.

At its core, FOMO is social anxiety driven by the perception that others might be having fulfilling experiences from which one is absent. This anxiety manifests from a primal instinct – the need to belong. Our ancestors, who were hunter-gatherers, survived and thrived through community living. Being part of the tribe meant protection, shared resources, and increased chances of survival. Missing out on vital information or events could be detrimental, and over time, this evolved into an instinctual fear.

Fast forward to the 21st century, this primitive fear has found a new arena – the digital world. Social media, with its incessant barrage of notifications about friends' vacations, gourmet meals, relationship milestones, and professional successes, provides constant glimpses into others' lives. This amplifies our inherent fear of exclusion, making us wonder if we're missing out on something better.

In India, a country with one of the world's largest youth populations and fastest-growing internet users, FOMO is more relevant than ever. Urban Indian youth are heavily influenced by global trends, and their increasing online presence makes them especially susceptible to FOMO. The barrage of Instagram stories featuring exotic vacations, the LinkedIn updates of friends landing prestigious internships, or the constant stream of WhatsApp group messages discussing the latest Netflix binge-watch – all contribute to an overwhelming sense that everyone else is leading a more exciting life.

FOMO isn't just an idle worry about missing out on a friend's party or not being part of a trending meme. It can lead to a constant state of unease, dissatisfaction, and restlessness. Being aware of its origins and understanding its presence in our lives is the first step toward tackling this pervasive phenomenon.

The Role of Technology: How Social Media and the Digital Age Intensify FOMO

Technology, particularly social media, has become a double-edged sword in our lives. On one hand, it connects us with the world, democratizes information, and opens doors to opportunities. On the other hand, it creates an environment ripe for comparison, envy, and FOMO. The constant connectivity and infinite scrolling have exacerbated our fear of missing out, turning it into a chronic condition rather than a fleeting worry.

Social media platforms operate on an 'always on' culture, providing a never-ending stream of updates from our peers and influencers, painting a picture of an idealized world that most can only aspire to. The curated glimpses into their seemingly perfect lives can trigger a sense of inadequacy and FOMO.

In India, with its burgeoning tech-savvy population, the impact of this digital bombardment is palpable. The youth are driven to continuously stay 'plugged in', for the fear of missing out can be overwhelming. From missing an important update on an online class to being out of the loop in the latest social media trend, FOMO seeps into every aspect of the digital life of the Indian Gen Z.

FOMO and the Indian Millennial: A Closer Look at the Cultural Factors at Play

In the context of India, FOMO takes on a unique cultural hue. For a society steeped in tradition, where success is often measured by societal standards of wealth, education, and status, FOMO isn't just about missing out on experiences but also about lagging in the race to societal validation. This is particularly true for the millennials, who are caught in the crosshairs of tradition and modernity.

Indian millennials, influenced by global trends, yet rooted in their cultural ethos, grapple with FOMO on multiple fronts. The pressure to excel academically, the quest to secure a stable job, and the societal expectations to marry and settle down at a certain age, all intersect with their aspirations and the desire to lead an experientially rich life.

The advent of start-up culture and success stories of young entrepreneurs like Ritesh Agarwal of OYO Rooms or Bhavish Aggarwal of Ola Cabs add to this complex mix. The tantalizing possibility of breaking away from the conventional path and achieving meteoric success can be both inspiring and anxiety-inducing.

Therefore, understanding FOMO and its impact on Indian millennials and Gen Z involves recognizing this delicate interplay of societal expectations, personal aspirations, and the influence of the digital age. The first step towards managing FOMO lies in comprehending its multifaceted nature in the Indian context.

The Power of the Present Moment: Why Immersing Ourselves Fully in the Now is a Powerful Antidote to FOMO

In the relentless pursuit of the future and the regret of the past, we often lose sight of the only real moment we have the present. The frenetic pace of modern life, compounded by the constant digital distractions, can create a disconnect with our present reality, fueling our FOMO. However, finding ways to reconnect with the here and now can be a potent antidote to this pervasive fear.

The concept of mindfulness, deeply rooted in Eastern philosophies and now popularized globally, is a powerful tool in our arsenal against FOMO. Mindfulness, put simply, is the practice of being fully present in the current moment, acknowledging and accepting our thoughts, feelings, and sensations without judgment.

By practicing mindfulness, we train ourselves to stop ruminating over past events or obsessing about the future.

This focus on the present moment helps quell the anxieties bred by FOMO. When we're truly present, we don't feel the need to compare our lives with others, nor do we feel anxious about missing out. Instead, we learn to value and appreciate our current experiences and realities.

For Indian Gen Z, this can be particularly empowering. TD is connecting from the digital world, even for a few minutes each day, can foster a stronger connection with the self and the immediate surroundings. Practicing mindfulness could mean savoring a cup of chai without scrolling through Instagram, or simply observing the hustle and bustle of the city on a rickshaw ride without feeling the need to capture it for Snapchat.

Being present allows us to engage more deeply with our experiences, to find joy and fulfillment in them, and, most importantly, to realize that each person's journey is unique, and comparing it to others only robs us of our happiness. By choosing to be fully present, we can reclaim control over our experiences and reduce the pervasive sense of FOMO.

Mindfulness in the Indian Context: The Confluence of Modern Psychology and Ancient Wisdom

The practice of mindfulness, while enjoying a resurgence in popularity globally due to its scientifically validated benefits, is far from being a new concept. It finds its roots in the ancient philosophies of India. The understanding and application of mindfulness present a beautiful confluence of modern psychology and India's ancient wisdom.

At the heart of many Indian traditions and philosophies such as Yoga and Buddhism, the practice of being mindful, of fostering an intimate connection with the present moment, has been emphasized for centuries. The wisdom encapsulated in these age-old practices provides practical tools for managing the vicissitudes of the human mind and overcoming anxieties like FOMO.

While mindfulness may seem somewhat alien to the smartphone-toting, Instagram-scrolling Indian Gen Z, they might be surprised to find that it already subtly weaves itself into the fabric of their daily lives. The familiar rituals of lighting a diya in the evening, engaging in the rhythmic routines of yoga, or even the act of kneading dough for roti— all these practices, when done with attention and intention, become acts of mindfulness. These rituals passed down through generations, are India's very own stress-busters, waiting to be recognized and embraced in their full potency.

In recent years, several Indian startups have begun leveraging technology to deliver mindfulness training. Apps like Headspace and Calm have been localized, making mindfulness practices more accessible to Indian millennials and Gen Z. They are creating platforms that integrate traditional Indian practices with modern psychological understandings, aiming to help users combat stress and FOMO while embracing the present moment.

From Theory to Practice: Practical and Accessible Mindfulness Techniques for Daily Life

i. **Mindful Breathing:** The cornerstone of mindfulness is observing one's breath. Mindful breathing involves focusing on the sensation of breath entering and leaving your nostrils, or the rise and fall of your chest or abdomen. When your mind wanders, and it will gently steer it back to your breath without self-judgment. Regular practice, even for a few minutes a day, can significantly reduce anxiety and promote a sense of calm.

ii. **Body Scan:** This technique involves paying attention to different parts of your body, from your toes to your head, and observing sensations without judgment. It cultivates a heightened awareness of the body and can reveal a lot about our emotional state. It also aids in releasing tension and promoting relaxation.

iii. **Mindful Eating:** We often eat our meals while being preoccupied with our screens, completely detached from the experience of eating. Mindful eating involves truly savoring your food - observing the colors, smelling the aroma, tasting the flavors, and chewing slowly. It can enhance the pleasure of eating and also promotes healthier eating habits.

iv. **Walking Meditation:** Instead of walking while lost in thoughts or glued to our screens, mindful walking involves being fully present during the walk. Feel the ground beneath your feet, observe the surroundings, and pay attention to your body's movement. It's an excellent way of cultivating mindfulness and can be integrated into our daily lives easily.

v. **Mindful Listening:** In a world of noise and constant chatter, we often listen to respond rather than understand. Mindful listening involves truly hearing what is being said, without planning a response or passing judgment. It can vastly improve our relationships and help us understand others better.

Each of these techniques can be an effective antidote to FOMO. By grounding us in the present moment, they diminish the tendency to look over the fence, cultivating contentment and serenity in the process.

Chapter 13

Entitlement – The World Owes Me Nothing

Welcome to a world where the "me" overshadows the "we," where demands drown out gratitude, and expectations often tower above empathy. In this world, entitlement reigns supreme. Entitlement is the belief that one is inherently deserving of special treatment or certain privileges, regardless of effort or contribution. It's like waiting for the fruit without nurturing the tree, a mindset that expects rewards without the necessary toil. A pervasive attitude, it has woven its way into various aspects of modern life - from individual interactions to group dynamics, from work settings to intimate relationships.

The Global Entanglement with Entitlement: Unraveling the Socio-cultural Threads

Entitlement is not a standalone phenomenon; it is intricately linked to the socio-cultural fabric of our times. We live in an era where immediate gratification is the norm. From fast-food to streaming platforms, everything is geared towards instant satisfaction. This culture of "instant everything" has a significant role in propagating the belief of 'deservedness' without commensurate effort.

Moreover, the rise of consumerism, the increasing emphasis on individualism, and the intense competition created by global capitalism further stoke the flames of entitlement. When these macro factors converge with micro factors like parental indulgence or a lack of discipline during formative years, the 'world owes me' mindset thrives.

Notably, while entitlement is a global phenomenon, its manifestations vary across different societies and cultures. As we delve deeper into the Indian context, it's essential to recognize the unique sociocultural variables that contribute to its emergence and evolution in the Subcontinent.

The Entitlement Quake in Personal Relationships: When Fault Lines of Privilege Erode Bonds

The insidious tendrils of entitlement can cause havoc in the lush gardens of personal relationships. When one person in a relationship operates from a standpoint of entitlement, it disturbs the delicate balance of give and take, creating tremors that can eventually lead to fractures.

At the heart of healthy relationships lies reciprocity - a mutual exchange of affection, respect, and support. However, the entitlement mindset breeds an unequal dynamic, where one person's wants and needs are continually prioritized above the other's. It becomes a one-sided transaction, with the entitled individual behaving like a relentless debtor, expecting constant payments of attention, validation, and effort without a reciprocal investment.

This skewed dynamic sows seeds of resentment and dissatisfaction. It's akin to a seesaw that's perpetually tilted to one side, disrupting the rhythm of balanced interaction and mutual enjoyment. The other person can feel unheard, unappreciated, and even used, leading to an emotional disconnect that weakens the relationship over time.

The impact is especially profound in familial relationships and friendships, where informality and closeness can sometimes be misused by the entitled individual to take others for granted. The effects ripple through the relationship ecosystem, creating discord and discontent.

As we walk further down this path, it becomes apparent that unchecked entitlement doesn't merely strain relationships, it risks breaking them. Understanding these impacts is the first step towards recalibrating our expectations and rebalancing our relationships. In the upcoming sections, we will explore how to combat entitlement and nurture healthier interpersonal dynamics rooted in empathy, respect, and mutual reciprocity.

Entitlement in the Workplace: The Silent Saboteur of Team Dynamics and Leadership

Beyond the personal realm, entitlement acts as an invisible saboteur in professional settings as well, distorting team dynamics and corroding leadership. The workplace is a melting pot of diverse personalities, skills, and experiences - a fertile ground for collaboration and collective growth. Yet, when entitlement seeps into this mix, it triggers a domino effect of disruptions that can impede productivity and dampen morale.

An entitled employee can create an uneven landscape, demanding more than their fair share of resources, recognition, and opportunities, while contributing less. They may insist on privileges without corresponding responsibilities or expect promotions and perks without demonstrating the requisite performance or growth. This "rights without responsibilities" attitude undermines the fundamental principles of fairness and meritocracy that propel a healthy, thriving work environment.

Such behavior doesn't just strain relationships with peers, but can also breed resentment and discord within a team. It's as if a single ill-tuned instrument is distorting the symphony of synergy, creating dissonance in place of harmony. The consequences are manifold - from declined team cohesiveness to reduced productivity and increased workplace conflict.

In a leadership role, entitlement morphs into autocracy. An entitled leader may assert their authority without acknowledging the team's input, stifle creativity by resisting diverse perspectives, or misuse power for personal gain. Such leadership not only corrodes team morale but also quashes innovation and growth. It's akin to a shadow that dims the vibrant palette of ideas, talent, and motivation within a team.

As the threads of entitlement weave through the fabric of professional settings, they unravel the tightly knit patterns of cooperation, respect, and shared success. Recognizing these ripple effects is pivotal to fostering an environment that champions mutual respect, equitable opportunities, and shared accountability. Moving forward, we'll delve into strategies that foster responsibility and empathy, displacing entitlement from our professional lives.

From Me to We: Fostering Responsibility and a Collective Mindset

Challenging the entitlement mindset begins with promoting a sense of responsibility and nurturing a collective consciousness. Responsibility is the antithesis of entitlement, it's about recognizing our obligations towards others, rather than focusing solely on our rights and privileges. It forms the bedrock of mutual respect, reciprocity, and collaboration.

But how does one foster responsibility? Especially in a generation that is often maligned for being self-centered. The key lies in shifting the perspective from 'Me' to 'We'. This shift isn't about disregarding personal aspirations or needs. It's about acknowledging that our actions and decisions reverberate beyond ourselves, impacting the collective whole.

In personal relationships, it could mean taking accountability for one's actions and their impact on others. It's about understanding that a healthy relationship is a two-way street, requiring mutual respect, compromise, and contribution. For instance, rather than assuming your friend will always be the one to adjust their schedule for a meet-up, show mutual respect by making an effort to accommodate their convenience as well.

In the professional sphere, cultivating responsibility could involve recognizing that every role, however minor it may appear, is integral to the overall success of the team. It's about valuing the collective goal above personal gain. A software engineer, for example, might be tempted to rush through the testing process to finish a project quickly.

However, considering the potential bugs that could later cause issues for others on the team, the responsible action would be to invest the necessary time in the testing phase.

Encouragingly, several Indian startups have started to foster this 'We' mindset by embracing flat organizational structures, where every team member feels responsible for the company's success. Flipkart, a leading Indian e-commerce giant, is an excellent example. By cultivating a culture that values each employee's contribution and encourages shared responsibility, they have managed to create a team deeply invested in the company's vision and success.

Promoting responsibility isn't just about prescribing a list of dos and don'ts. It's about creating an environment that values collective success over individual triumph, respects every contribution, and recognizes the interdependence of its members. It's about steering the ship from 'Me' to 'We'.

The Role of Empathy: Shattering the Entitlement Bubble

Empathy, the ability to understand and share the feelings of another, is a crucial tool in combatting the sense of entitlement. Entitlement, with its focus on self-centered desires and disregard for others' needs, thrives in an empathy-devoid environment. On the contrary, empathy encourages us to step outside of our comfort zones, to see the world from perspectives other than our own, thus effectively puncturing the entitlement bubble.

In personal relationships, empathy fosters compassion and understanding, mitigating the risk of conflicts that stem from a heightened sense of entitlement. It nudges us to listen to others, to appreciate their struggles and perspectives, and to respond with kindness. Consider a common scenario in Indian households, where traditionally, domestic chores have been primarily the woman's responsibility. A husband, who feels entitled to leisure after work, might disregard the exhaustive work his wife does at home. Here, empathy can play a transformative role. By stepping into his wife's shoes, and understanding her daily ordeals, he might become more appreciative of her efforts and consider sharing the household responsibilities.

Similarly, in professional settings, empathy can help build more collaborative and respectful environments. It helps leaders understand their team members' viewpoints, acknowledge their challenges, and respond more effectively. This approach nurtures a sense of being valued and heard, which in turn motivates employees and strengthens team dynamics. A case in point is the empathetic leadership demonstrated by the CEO of Zomato, a leading Indian food delivery service, during the pandemic. When faced with business uncertainty and potential layoffs, the CEO took a 100% salary cut to reduce the financial burden on the company and its employees, setting an empathetic example for others to follow.

Moreover, Gen Z, with its increasingly global outlook and exposure, has a unique opportunity to practice empathy on a wider scale. By engaging with diverse cultures, perspectives, and challenges, both offline and online, they can break free from the insular entitlement bubble and develop a more inclusive and compassionate worldview.

Thus, fostering empathy is not just about promoting kinder individuals but also about building more understanding and harmonious societies. As we cultivate this skill, we begin to see that the world does not owe us anything, but we owe the world our understanding and respect.

Emotional Intelligence: Navigating the Route to Decipher and Dissolve Entitlement

Emotional intelligence, as defined by psychologist Daniel Goleman, is the ability to understand and manage our own emotions and those of the people around us. It's an arsenal of skills comprising self-awareness, self-regulation, motivation, empathy, and social skills. These components serve as a robust counterforce to entitlement, providing a pathway to understand and overcome it.

Self-Awareness and Self-Regulation: These two aspects of emotional intelligence involve recognizing our emotions and controlling how we react to them. Entitlement often stems from an uncontrolled desire for more, fueled by feelings of inadequacy or superiority. To counter this, we must become aware of when we're feeling entitled and regulate our reactions. Consider a student who feels entitled to a perfect grade without putting in adequate effort. Here, self-awareness would mean acknowledging this unjust expectation, while self-regulation would involve tempering it with the reality that grades are a result of hard work and dedication.

Motivation: Motivation, another aspect of emotional intelligence, is about being driven to achieve for the sake of achievement. Entitlement can blur this, leading to a fixation on rewards rather than the joy of accomplishment.

A counteractive approach would be to focus on intrinsic motivation. Take the example of India's chess prodigy, Grandmaster Vidit Gujrathi. Despite his early success, he's known for his undying thirst for knowledge and constant improvement, embodying intrinsic motivation and debunking the myth of entitled success.

Empathy and Social Skills: These traits help us understand and respond appropriately to others' emotions, fostering healthier relationships. In an entitled mindset, one may overlook others' feelings and rights. To break free from this, we need to empathize with others and respond with kindness and respect. Indian cricket icon, Sachin Tendulkar's career offers a lesson here. Despite his staggering success, he's remembered as much for his humility and respect for colleagues and opponents, as for his cricketing prowess, a testament to his emotional intelligence.

In a nutshell, emotional intelligence can guide us to a deeper understanding of ourselves and others, enabling us to navigate the pitfalls of entitlement and cultivate healthier, more fulfilling relationships. This journey, albeit challenging, promises a profound shift from the confines of self-centeredness to the expansiveness of shared growth and success.

Sourcing from the Reservoir of Indian Wisdom: Timeless Tenets that Cultivate Humility and Gratitude

India, with its rich tapestry of cultural wisdom and ancient philosophies, holds a treasure trove of values that inherently nurture humility and gratitude, two antidotes to the venom of entitlement.

The Vedic Concept of 'Vasudhaiva Kutumbakam': This ancient Indian phrase translates to "The world is one family." It implores us to view every individual as part of a larger family - humanity itself. This perspective fosters a sense of interconnectedness and collective responsibility, dissolving the walls of entitlement. An example of this principle in action can be seen in the life of Abdul Kalam, the former President of India. Despite his high office, he always saw himself as a member of the broader human family, consistently prioritizing the welfare of the collective over personal gain.

The Practice of 'Seva': Seva, or selfless service, is another potent Indian concept that cultivates humility. It encourages serving others without expectation of reward or recognition, fostering humility and a sense of shared purpose. We see the embodiment of 'Seva' in the life of Sudha Murty, chairperson of Infosys Foundation. Her extensive philanthropic work, often conducted without fanfare, speaks volumes about her commitment to the spirit of Seva, a direct counter to entitlement.

Cultivating 'Santosha': Santosha, or contentment, is a principle from the yogic philosophy of Patanjali. It urges us to find contentment in what we have rather than constantly seeking more, cultivating a sense of gratitude. Indian Olympic medalist Mary Kom's story is the epitome of Santosha. Despite her humble beginnings, she found contentment in her passion for boxing, showing gratitude for her journey rather than entitlement for more fame or wealth.

Embracing 'Vinaya': Vinaya, translating to humility, is a core value across various Indian philosophies. It stresses the importance of being humble, regardless of one's achievements or stature. Vinaya can be observed in the life of India's "Metro Man" E. Sreedharan. Despite his monumental contributions to Indian infrastructure, his humility remains notable, countering any scope for entitlement.

These age-old Indian principles serve as potent anchors, grounding us in humility and gratitude and steering us away from the dangerous shores of entitlement. By embracing these values, we can foster healthier, more empathetic relationships, and create a more harmonious society.

Progressing Beyond the Entitlement Mindset for Personal Empowerment and Social Evolution

Beyond identifying entitlement and understanding its detrimental effects, we must also work towards consciously cultivating a mindset that challenges and moves beyond this destructive pattern of thought. This reframing process allows us to break free from the limiting cages of entitlement and instead tap into our potential for growth, leading to both personal empowerment and societal evolution.

The Power of Personal Responsibility: The first step in rewriting our narrative is accepting personal responsibility. When we understand that we are the architects of our lives, we shift from a passive stance, waiting for the world to meet our demands, to active engagement. This mindset propels us towards seeking solutions, taking initiative, and creating change, instead of indulging in blame games or self-pity.

Cultivating Gratitude: Recognizing and acknowledging the good in our lives is another powerful tool for countering entitlement. By consciously practicing gratitude, we move our focus from what we believe we're owed to appreciating what we already have. This shift in perspective promotes contentment, reduces resentment, and increases our capacity for empathy, further diminishing entitlement's hold on us.

Fostering Humility: Recognizing that we are part of a larger collective and that everyone, irrespective of their role or status, deserves respect and kindness, helps foster humility. This understanding can help dissolve the inflated sense of self-importance often associated with entitlement. Humility also opens us to learning and growth, as we acknowledge that we don't have all the answers and that others can offer valuable insights and wisdom.

Embracing Growth and Learning: Entitlement often leads to stagnation, as we rest on our laurels, believing we are already at our peak. By adopting a growth mindset, we acknowledge our capacity for continual learning and evolution. This mindset promotes curiosity, resilience, and perseverance, pushing us to strive for self-improvement rather than expecting the world to adapt to us.

By consciously choosing to adopt these perspectives and attitudes, we move beyond the limiting clutches of the entitlement mentality. Not only does this shift empower us as individuals, but it also paves the way for a more empathetic, harmonious, and progressive society. As we evolve from the 'me-centered' approach to a 'we-focused' one, we contribute towards building a more compassionate and equitable world.

Chapter 14

Revisiting the Voyage

Revisiting the Voyage – A Recap of the Central Themes and Insights

As we approach the conclusion of our enlightening journey, it's time to cast our gaze back over the wealth of wisdom we've gathered.

We began our journey by recognizing the distinct challenges facing the Gen-Z Indians, noting the necessity of a firm foundation for personal and professional development, and reconciling Indian cultural values with the demands of a modern, globalizing world.

In our exploration of perfectionism, we learned to understand its pitfalls and celebrate progress rather than unattainable perfection. We highlighted the importance of self-compassion and practical techniques to mitigate the ill effects of this relentless pursuit of perfection.

Our expedition into fear of failure revealed its transformative potential, turning perceived defeats into life's most valuable lessons. Through inspiring stories, we celebrated the brave individuals who have embraced failure as a stepping stone rather than an obstacle.

Addressing procrastination, we unearthed its root causes, equipped ourselves with time management strategies, and acknowledged the cultural influences on our tendencies to delay.

We also navigated the hazardous terrain of social comparison, examining its impacts on self-esteem and mental health. We underscored the importance of personal growth and gratitude, drawing inspiration from remarkable Indians who have managed to sidestep the comparison trap.

Our exploration led us to critically assess our relationship with technology, advocating for a balanced digital diet and emphasizing the importance of nurturing real-world connections in an increasingly virtual world.

As we delved into impostor syndrome, we unveiled techniques to conquer self-doubt and build self-confidence, drawing motivation from notable Indians who have triumphed over this uninvited mental guest.

The myth of multitasking was debunked as we promoted the benefits of focused attention and single-tasking, equipping ourselves with the tools for mindful living in a fast-paced world.

Our journey also carried us into the realm of conflict, where we developed a new appreciation for its constructive potential. We recognized the importance of effective communication skills and navigated the cultural norms that can sometimes hinder open dialogue.

We confronted the comfort zone, promoting the idea that real growth often lies on the other side of discomfort. Celebrating change and risk-taking, we drew inspiration from trailblazing Indians who dared to venture into the unknown.

As we challenged traditional markers of success, we encouraged the discovery of personal values and the crafting of a personally meaningful life. We celebrated those who dared to carve out their paths, redefining the Indian dream.

Finally, we addressed the perils of entitlement, underscoring the importance of responsibility, empathy, and emotional intelligence. We reflected on the traditional Indian values that promote humility and gratitude, providing a counterweight to a 'world owes me' mentality.

Now, standing at the threshold of conclusion, let us soak in these myriad lessons learned and embrace the distinctiveness of being a Gen-Z Indian. As we prepare for a fulfilling professional journey and a meaningful life, may these insights light our path, guiding us towards an existence that's vibrant, balanced, and deeply satisfying.

Gen-Z Indians stand at a unique cultural confluence, deftly balancing the traditions passed down through generations and the influences of an increasingly interconnected world. They are inheritors of a rich cultural heritage, which inculcates deep-rooted values and a unique perspective on life. At the same time, they are digital natives in a rapidly globalizing world, well-versed in the latest technological advancements and international trends. This juxtaposition of old and new provides them with a multi-faceted worldview that sets them apart.

The Dual Dance – Gen-Z Indians at the Crossroads of Heritage and Globalization

There is a vivid dance of dualities unfolding in the lives of Gen-Z Indians. On one side, they have inherited a rich cultural tapestry woven with age-old traditions, wisdom, and values. These inherited elements form a cornerstone of their identity, offering a robust framework that guides their life decisions, interpersonal relationships, and outlook toward the world. The quintessential Indian philosophy of unity in diversity, deep respect for elders, focus on community and family ties, and the art of finding contentment in simple pleasures, imbue them with a sense of grounding and continuity in a rapidly evolving world.

However, the dance doesn't end here. On the other side, Gen-Z Indians are thriving in the vibrant rhythm of the modern world. They are digital natives, born into an era of rapidly evolving technology that is reshaping the contours of human life. They effortlessly straddle the world of hashtags, apps, and global trends, utilizing these digital tools to broaden their horizons, forge global connections, and influence change on a wider scale. Their agility in adapting to technological advancements, their familiarity with the digital universe, and their ability to leverage these platforms to voice their opinions or propel social change amplify their potential on a global stage.

This intersection of tradition and modernity, heritage and globalization, renders the Gen-Z Indian unique. This dual dance endows them with a distinct perspective - one that is rooted in cultural wisdom yet attuned to global progress. They can view problems through a broader lens, devise innovative solutions that integrate traditional wisdom with modern science, and drive forward with a sense of purpose and vision that respects the past while embracing the future.

In essence, the Gen-Z Indians are dancing with balance on a tightrope suspended between their heritage and the influences of a globalized world. It is this balance that will enable them to leap into the future while staying connected to their roots, crafting a world that is a harmonious blend of the time-tested wisdom of their ancestors and the innovative spirit of the digital age.

The challenges encountered on this journey are diverse, reflecting the intricacies of Indian society. They range from societal expectations and pressure to conform to the struggle of defining one's identity amidst the cacophony of a multicultural nation. The traditional yardsticks of success are being challenged, and the line between personal and professional life is getting blurred in a digitalized world. Not to mention, they are the first generation to grapple with the twin beasts of information overload and digital distraction, which bring their own set of mental health issues and social challenges.

Despite these obstacles, every twist and turn in the labyrinth holds the potential for growth and evolution. The Gen-Z Indian, armed with their unique blend of traditional wisdom and digital savviness, is well-equipped to seize these opportunities. They are redefining the markers of success to align with their values, challenging societal norms that limit potential, and using technology as a tool for positive change. They are leveraging their diverse cultural heritage to foster inclusivity and mutual respect, thereby shaping a more empathetic and connected society.

Moreover, they are navigating this journey not as passive travelers but as active change-makers. They are utilizing digital platforms to amplify their voices, leading social movements, advocating for policy changes, and striving to create a more equitable world. In this quest, they are not only shaping their individual lives but also the collective future of the nation.

The journey of the Gen-Z Indians through the intricate terrain of modern society is a testament to their resilience, adaptability, and transformative potential. It is a journey marked by challenges and opportunities, with each step carving a path that is distinctively their own. As they continue to navigate this labyrinth, their journey holds valuable insights and lessons for all generations, reinforcing the belief that every challenge is an opportunity for growth, every setback a stepping stone to resilience, and every journey a story of transformation.

Unleashing the Force - Harnessing the Power and Potential of Gen-Z Indians to Craft the Future

The power of the Gen-Z Indian lies not just in their numbers, but in the profound potential they carry within. They stand at the helm of the future, poised to redefine the contours of the world as we know it. This isn't merely a prophetic statement but a palpable reality reflected in their thoughts, actions, and aspirations.

The Gen-Z Indian is inherently a divergent thinker, capable of challenging conventional norms and questioning established structures. Their worldview isn't shackled by a monolithic perspective but instead is dynamically shaped by a confluence of heritage and globalization. This multiplicity of influences and experiences nurtures their ability to envision a world that straddles the balance between preservation and progress.

Their digital fluency allows them to turn the challenges of the digital age into opportunities for advancement. They harness technology to foster connections, build communities, champion causes, and innovate solutions. Their tech-savviness isn't just a trait, but a tool that amplifies their impact and reaches, making them pivotal players in a global narrative.

Moreover, the Gen-Z Indian is not just a passive recipient of change but an active participant in its creation. They understand that their choices today are the building blocks of tomorrow. This proactive and forward-thinking approach is reflected in their commitment to issues like sustainability, equality, and social justice. They believe in a future that is inclusive, fair, and respectful and are willing to roll up their sleeves and work for it.

Most importantly, the power of the Gen-Z Indian lies in their authenticity and resilience. They aren't afraid to embrace their unique identities, voice their opinions, or stand their ground in the face of adversity. They are showing the world that being true to oneself isn't just an act of courage, but a catalyst for change.

As we prepare to pass the baton to the Gen-Z Indians, we can rest assured that it is in capable hands. Their journey might be rife with challenges, but they have proven time and again that they can rise to the occasion. They carry within them the promise and potential to craft a future that mirrors their vision - a future that is as diverse, dynamic, and resilient as they are. As they step into this role, the world watches with anticipation, for they are not just the leaders of tomorrow, but the architects of a future we are yet to imagine.

Meet the Author

Srinivas Saripalli is a seasoned business leader and an agile coach with over two decades of experience in various leadership roles in multinational corporations. He is also an Executive Leadership and Life Coach. As a fully trained and qualified NLP, Transformational, Leadership, and Life Coach, he has dedicated his career to unlocking human potential. Srinivas's life coaching sessions have transformed lives, leading to greater self-awareness and success. His latest work explores the challenges and triumphs of the visionary Gen-Z Indians, offering a roadmap to authenticity, resilience, and empowerment.

The author began his journey as a quality consultant, working closely with companies to assess their existing quality processes, identify gaps, and develop customized solutions. His keen analytical skills and attention to detail enabled him to effectively map out workflows, identify bottlenecks, and implement robust quality assurance measures. His recommendations and implementation strategies resulted in improved product quality, increased customer satisfaction, and enhanced overall operational efficiency.

Recognizing the need for agility in today's dynamic business landscape, the author transitioned into agile transformation consulting. With a deep understanding of agile principles and frameworks, he guided organizations through the adoption and implementation of agile methodologies such as Scrum, Kanban, and Lean. He coached teams and leaders on agile practices, facilitated effective collaboration, and fostered a culture of continuous improvement.

How the Author Became an Executive & Life Coach

For almost five years now, he has been a life coach, helping people around the world to get unstuck. As the Agile transitions & transformations in the Digital Age picked up, Mergers and Acquisitions grew bigger and employee issues became more complicated. He wanted to make sure he had all the skills to be able to deal with each person competently. He qualified as a Personal Performance Coach.

www.ingramcontent.com/pod-product-compliance
Lightning Source LLC
LaVergne TN
LVHW041104150826
845673LV00007B/1914
9798890677020